IMPACT
Daily Management of setting

Jigsaw
EARLY YEARS CONSULTANCY

This book will help you manage your early years settings numbers and ratios for every day

Love Team Jigsaw

INSTRUCTIONS

Every day

Before you leave your setting on a daily basis record how many children you have in for the next day including those that have English as an Additional Language and SEN. This will ensure you have a clear understanding and knowledge of ratios

Duty of Care

Jigsaw
EARLY YEARS CONSULTANCY

Date

Name of room	Age of room	Ratio in room
		:

Number of children in today	Number of children with EAL	Number of children with SEN	Number of 2 year old funded children	Number of 3 year old funded children

Staffing

Name of Staff	Qualifications	First Aid trained ✓	Safeguarding trained ✓
		◯	◯
		◯	◯
		◯	◯
		◯	◯
		◯	◯
		◯	◯

Jigsaw
EARLY YEARS CONSULTANCY

Date

Name of room

Age of room

Ratio in room

Number of children in today	Number of children with EAL	Number of children with SEN	Number of 2 year old funded children	Number of 3 year old funded children

Staffing

Name of Staff	Qualifications	First Aid trained ✓	Safeguarding trained ✓

Date

Name of room

Age of room

Ratio in room

:

Number of children in today

Number of children with EAL

Number of children with SEN

Number of 2 year old funded children

Number of 3 year old funded children

Staffing

Name of Staff	Qualifications	First Aid trained ✓	Safeguarding trained ✓
		◯	◯
		◯	◯
		◯	◯
		◯	◯
		◯	◯
		◯	◯

Jigsaw
EARLY YEARS CONSULTANCY

Date

Name of room

Age of room

Ratio in room

Number of children in today	Number of children with EAL	Number of children with SEN	Number of 2 year old funded children	Number of 3 year old funded children

Staffing

Name of Staff	Qualifications	First Aid trained ✓	Safeguarding trained ✓
		○	○
		○	○
		○	○
		○	○
		○	○
		○	○

Date

Name of room	Age of room	Ratio in room
		:

Number of children in today	Number of children with EAL	Number of children with SEN	Number of 2 year old funded children	Number of 3 year old funded children

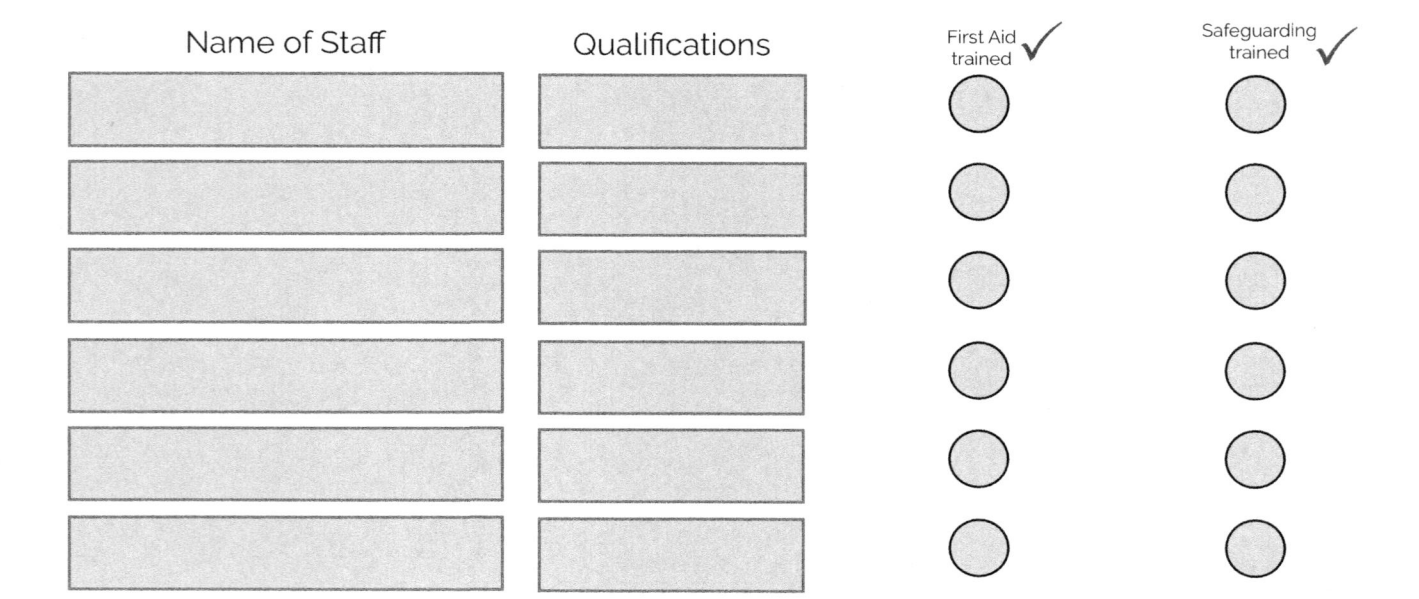

Staffing

Name of Staff	Qualifications	First Aid trained ✓	Safeguarding trained ✓
		○	○
		○	○
		○	○
		○	○
		○	○
		○	○

Date

Name of room	Age of room	Ratio in room
		:

Number of children in today	Number of children with EAL	Number of children with SEN	Number of 2 year old funded children	Number of 3 year old funded children

Staffing

Name of Staff	Qualifications	First Aid trained ✓	Safeguarding trained ✓

Jigsaw
EARLY YEARS CONSULTANCY

Date

Name of room	Age of room	Ratio in room
		:

Number of children in today	Number of children with EAL	Number of children with SEN	Number of 2 year old funded children	Number of 3 year old funded children

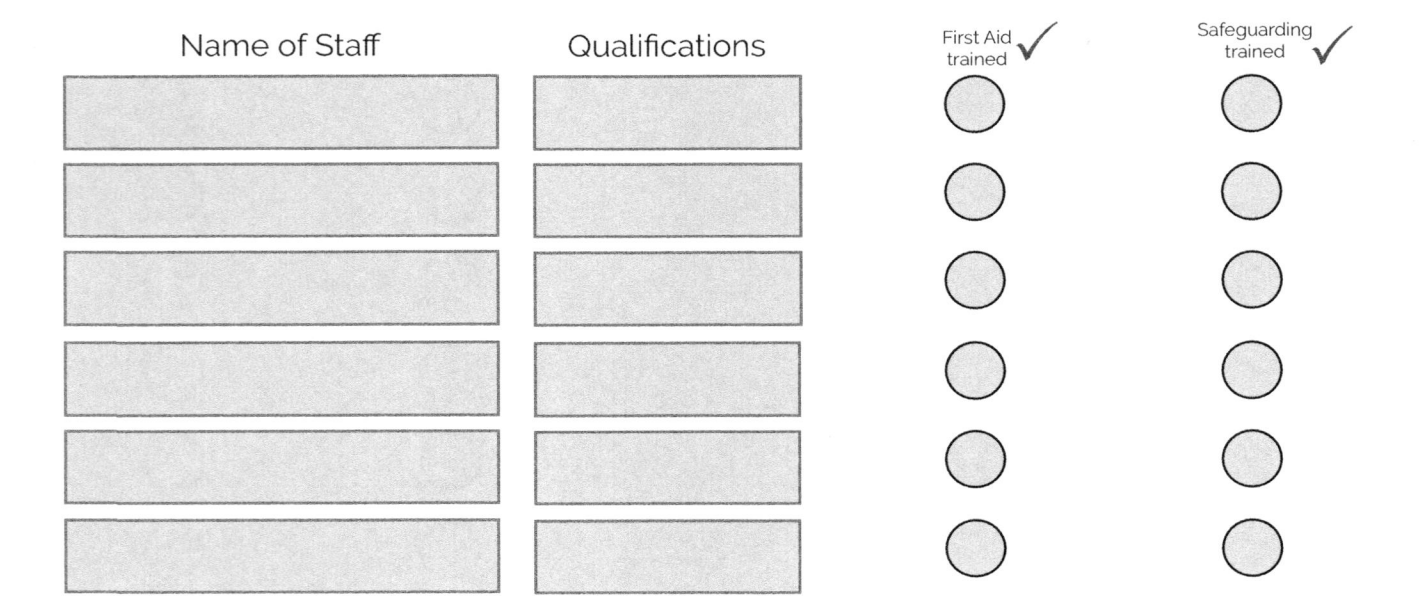

Staffing

Name of Staff	Qualifications	First Aid trained ✓	Safeguarding trained ✓
		○	○
		○	○
		○	○
		○	○
		○	○
		○	○

Date

Name of room	Age of room	Ratio in room
		:

Number of children in today	Number of children with EAL	Number of children with SEN	Number of 2 year old funded children	Number of 3 year old funded children

Staffing

Name of Staff	Qualifications	First Aid trained ✓	Safeguarding trained ✓
		○	○
		○	○
		○	○
		○	○
		○	○
		○	○

Date

Name of room

Age of room

Ratio in room

:

Number of children in today

Number of children with EAL

Number of children with SEN

Number of 2 year old funded children

Number of 3 year old funded children

Staffing

Name of Staff	Qualifications	First Aid trained ✓	Safeguarding trained ✓

Date

Name of room

Age of room

Ratio in room

Number of children in today	Number of children with EAL	Number of children with SEN	Number of 2 year old funded children	Number of 3 year old funded children

Staffing

Name of Staff	Qualifications	First Aid trained ✓	Safeguarding trained ✓
		○	○
		○	○
		○	○
		○	○
		○	○
		○	○

Jigsaw
EARLY YEARS CONSULTANCY

Date

Name of room	Age of room	Ratio in room
		:

Number of children in today	Number of children with EAL	Number of children with SEN	Number of 2 year old funded children	Number of 3 year old funded children

Staffing

Name of Staff	Qualifications	First Aid trained ✓	Safeguarding trained ✓
		○	○
		○	○
		○	○
		○	○
		○	○
		○	○

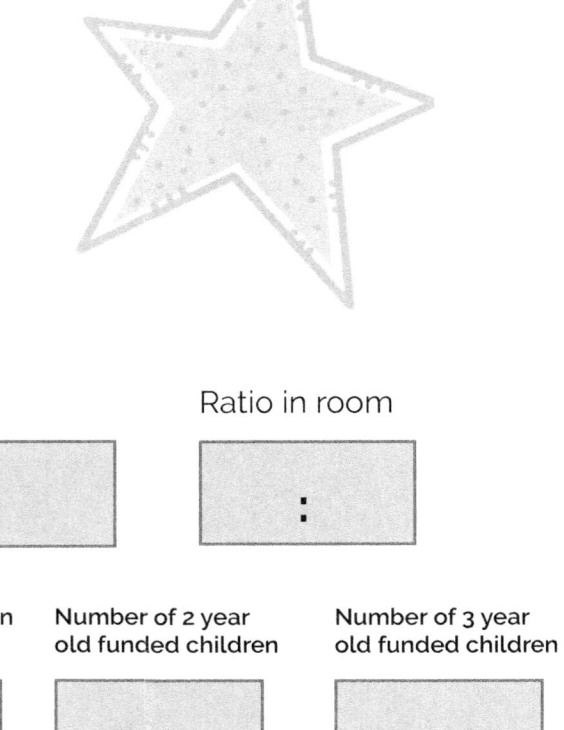

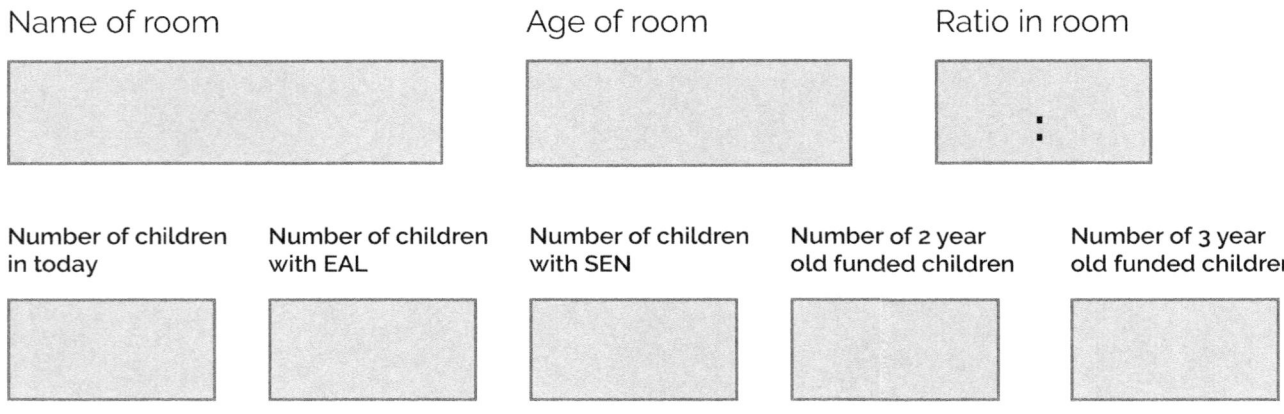

Jigsaw
EARLY YEARS CONSULTANCY

Date

Name of room	Age of room	Ratio in room
		:

Number of children in today	Number of children with EAL	Number of children with SEN	Number of 2 year old funded children	Number of 3 year old funded children

Staffing

Name of Staff	Qualifications	First Aid trained ✓	Safeguarding trained ✓

Date

Name of room	Age of room	Ratio in room
		:

Number of children in today	Number of children with EAL	Number of children with SEN	Number of 2 year old funded children	Number of 3 year old funded children

Staffing

Name of Staff	Qualifications	First Aid trained ✓	Safeguarding trained ✓
		◯	◯
		◯	◯
		◯	◯
		◯	◯
		◯	◯
		◯	◯

Date

Name of room

Age of room

Ratio in room

Number of children in today

Number of children with EAL

Number of children with SEN

Number of 2 year old funded children

Number of 3 year old funded children

Staffing

Name of Staff	Qualifications	First Aid trained ✓	Safeguarding trained ✓

Jigsaw
EARLY YEARS CONSULTANCY

Date

Name of room	Age of room	Ratio in room
		:

Number of children in today	Number of children with EAL	Number of children with SEN	Number of 2 year old funded children	Number of 3 year old funded children

Staffing

Name of Staff	Qualifications	First Aid trained ✓	Safeguarding trained ✓
		○	○
		○	○
		○	○
		○	○
		○	○
		○	○

Date

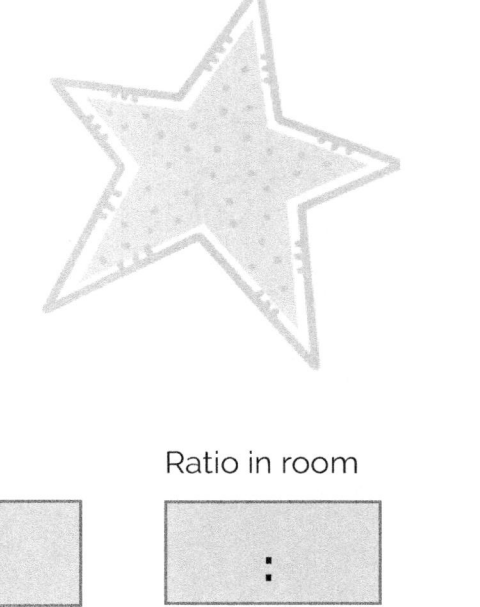

Name of room	Age of room	Ratio in room
		:

Number of children in today	Number of children with EAL	Number of children with SEN	Number of 2 year old funded children	Number of 3 year old funded children

Staffing

Name of Staff	Qualifications	First Aid trained ✓	Safeguarding trained ✓

Date

Name of room

Age of room

Ratio in room
:

Number of children in today

Number of children with EAL

Number of children with SEN

Number of 2 year old funded children

Number of 3 year old funded children

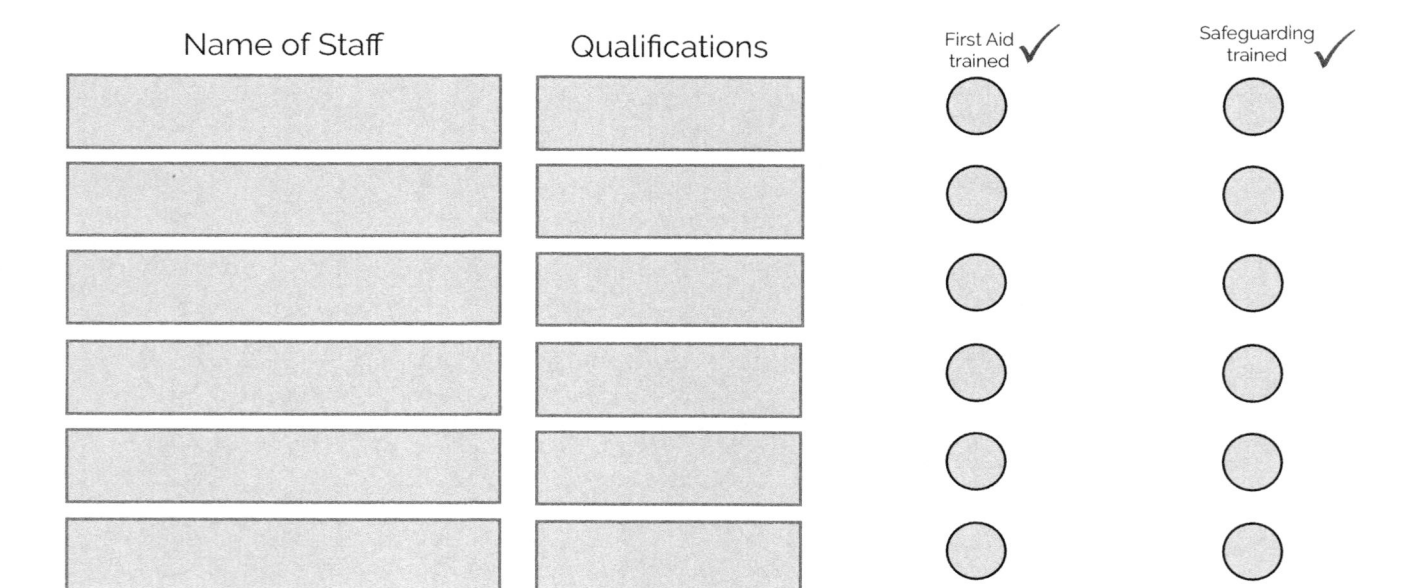

Staffing

Name of Staff	Qualifications	First Aid trained ✓	Safeguarding trained ✓

Date

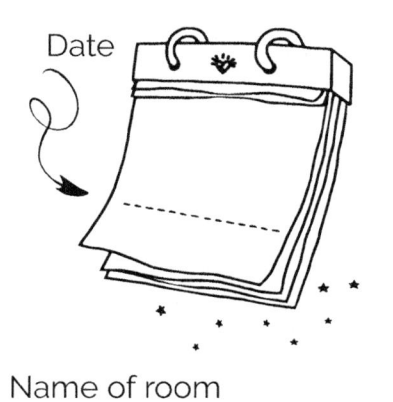

Name of room

Age of room

Ratio in room

Number of children in today	Number of children with EAL	Number of children with SEN	Number of 2 year old funded children	Number of 3 year old funded children

Staffing

Name of Staff	Qualifications	First Aid trained ✓	Safeguarding trained ✓

Date

Name of room

Age of room

Ratio in room

:

Number of children in today

Number of children with EAL

Number of children with SEN

Number of 2 year old funded children

Number of 3 year old funded children

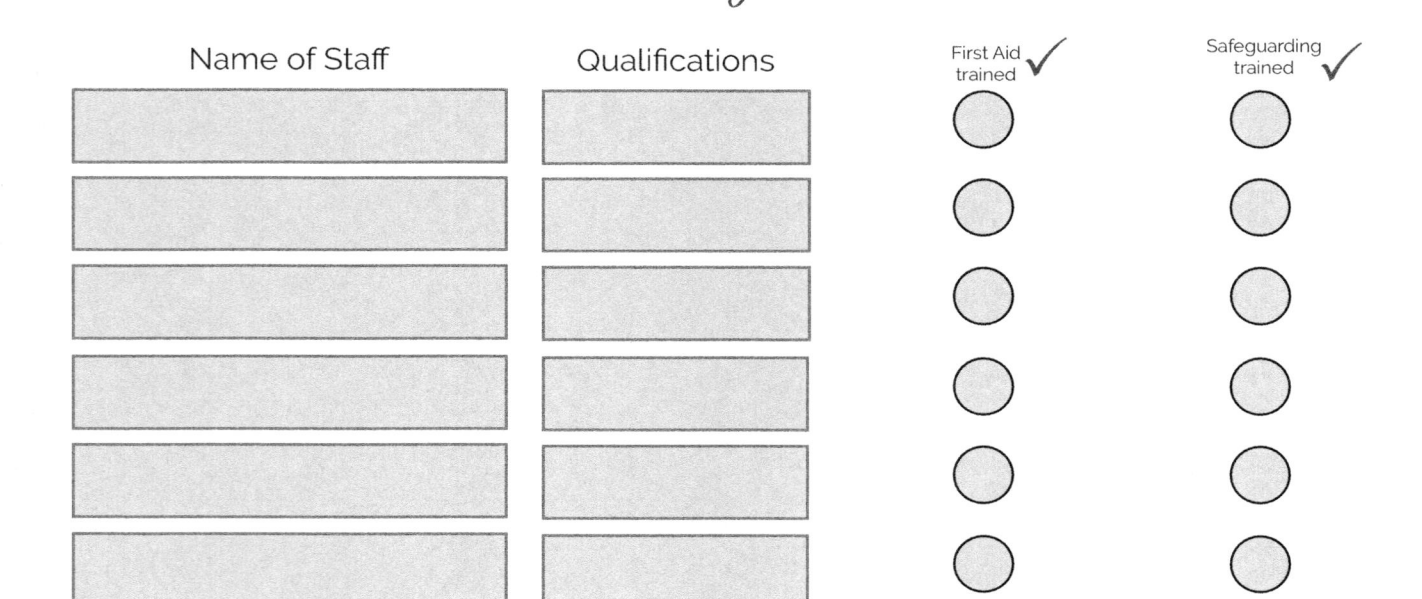

Staffing

Name of Staff	Qualifications	First Aid trained ✓	Safeguarding trained ✓
		○	○
		○	○
		○	○
		○	○
		○	○
		○	○

Jigsaw
EARLY YEARS CONSULTANCY

Date

Name of room	Age of room	Ratio in room
		:

Number of children in today	Number of children with EAL	Number of children with SEN	Number of 2 year old funded children	Number of 3 year old funded children

Staffing

Name of Staff	Qualifications	First Aid trained ✓	Safeguarding trained ✓
		◯	◯
		◯	◯
		◯	◯
		◯	◯
		◯	◯
		◯	◯

Jigsaw
EARLY YEARS CONSULTANCY

Date

Name of room	Age of room	Ratio in room
		:

Number of children in today	Number of children with EAL	Number of children with SEN	Number of 2 year old funded children	Number of 3 year old funded children

Staffing

Name of Staff	Qualifications	First Aid trained ✓	Safeguarding trained ✓
		○	○
		○	○
		○	○
		○	○
		○	○
		○	○

Date

Name of room

Age of room

Ratio in room

Number of children in today

Number of children with EAL

Number of children with SEN

Number of 2 year old funded children

Number of 3 year old funded children

Staffing

Name of Staff	Qualifications	First Aid trained ✓	Safeguarding trained ✓
		○	○
		○	○
		○	○
		○	○
		○	○
		○	○

Date

Name of room	Age of room	Ratio in room
		:

Number of children in today	Number of children with EAL	Number of children with SEN	Number of 2 year old funded children	Number of 3 year old funded children

Staffing

Name of Staff	Qualifications	First Aid trained ✓	Safeguarding trained ✓
		○	○
		○	○
		○	○
		○	○
		○	○
		○	○

Jigsaw
EARLY YEARS CONSULTANCY

Date

Name of room	Age of room	Ratio in room
		:

Number of children in today	Number of children with EAL	Number of children with SEN	Number of 2 year old funded children	Number of 3 year old funded children

Staffing

Name of Staff	Qualifications	First Aid trained ✓	Safeguarding trained ✓
		○	○
		○	○
		○	○
		○	○
		○	○
		○	○

Jigsaw
EARLY YEARS CONSULTANCY

Date

Name of room

Age of room

Ratio in room

:

Number of children in today

Number of children with EAL

Number of children with SEN

Number of 2 year old funded children

Number of 3 year old funded children

Staffing

Name of Staff	Qualifications	First Aid trained ✓	Safeguarding trained ✓

Jigsaw
EARLY YEARS CONSULTANCY

Date

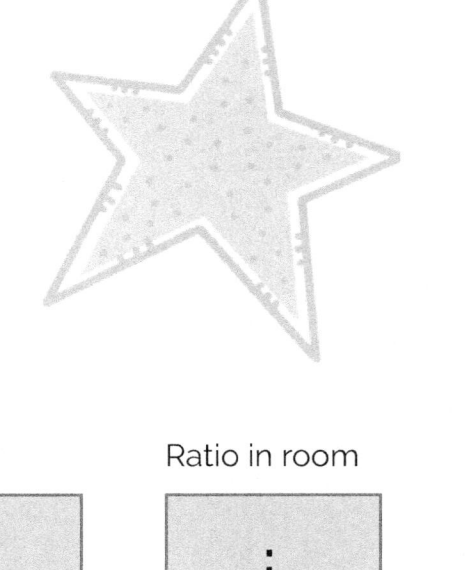

Name of room	Age of room	Ratio in room
		:

Number of children in today	Number of children with EAL	Number of children with SEN	Number of 2 year old funded children	Number of 3 year old funded children

Staffing

Name of Staff	Qualifications	First Aid trained ✓	Safeguarding trained ✓
		○	○
		○	○
		○	○
		○	○
		○	○
		○	○

Jigsaw
EARLY YEARS CONSULTANCY

Date

Name of room	Age of room	Ratio in room
		:

Number of children in today	Number of children with EAL	Number of children with SEN	Number of 2 year old funded children	Number of 3 year old funded children

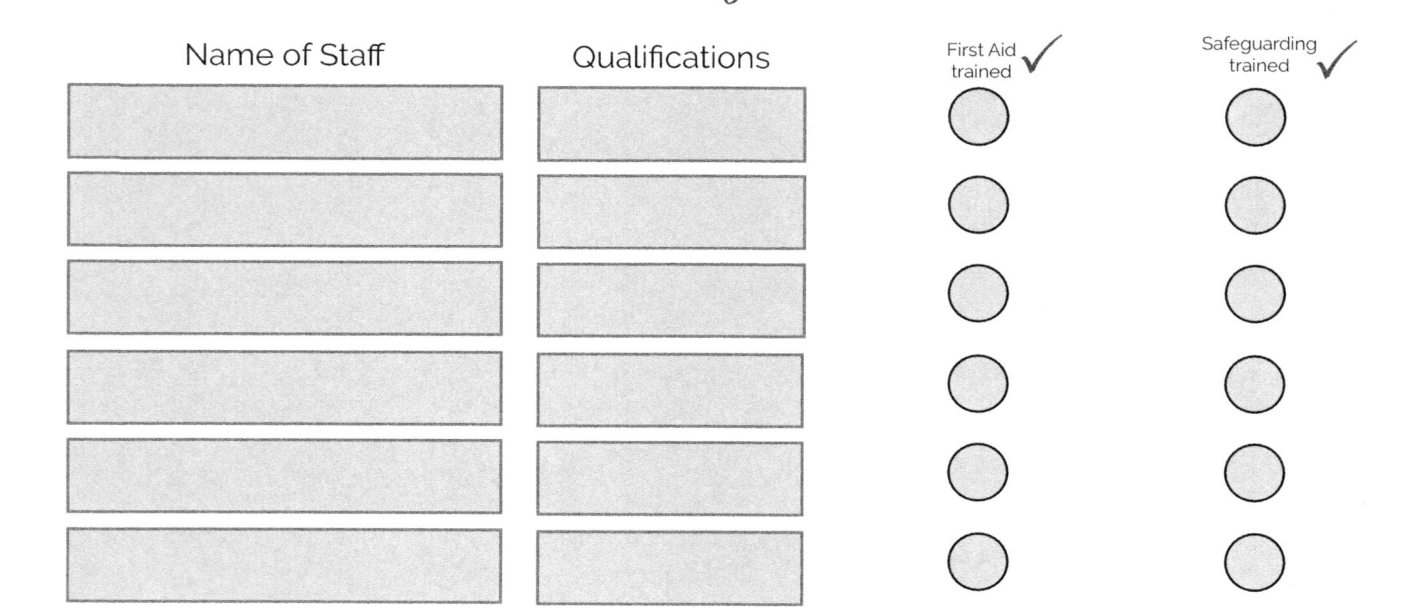

Staffing

Name of Staff	Qualifications	First Aid trained ✓	Safeguarding trained ✓
		○	○
		○	○
		○	○
		○	○
		○	○
		○	○

Date

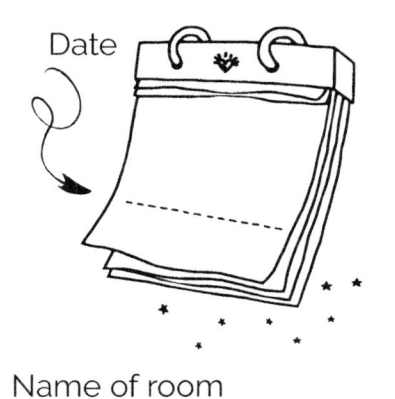

Jigsaw
EARLY YEARS CONSULTANCY

Name of room	Age of room	Ratio in room
		:

Number of children in today	Number of children with EAL	Number of children with SEN	Number of 2 year old funded children	Number of 3 year old funded children

Staffing

Name of Staff	Qualifications	First Aid trained ✓	Safeguarding trained ✓
		○	○
		○	○
		○	○
		○	○
		○	○
		○	○

Date

Name of room	Age of room	Ratio in room
		:

Number of children in today	Number of children with EAL	Number of children with SEN	Number of 2 year old funded children	Number of 3 year old funded children

Staffing

Name of Staff	Qualifications	First Aid trained ✓	Safeguarding trained ✓
		◯	◯
		◯	◯
		◯	◯
		◯	◯
		◯	◯
		◯	◯

Date

Name of room

Age of room

Ratio in room

Number of children in today

Number of children with EAL

Number of children with SEN

Number of 2 year old funded children

Number of 3 year old funded children

Staffing

Name of Staff	Qualifications	First Aid trained ✓	Safeguarding trained ✓

Date

Name of room

Age of room

Ratio in room

Number of children in today	Number of children with EAL	Number of children with SEN	Number of 2 year old funded children	Number of 3 year old funded children

Staffing

Name of Staff	Qualifications	First Aid trained ✓	Safeguarding trained ✓

Date

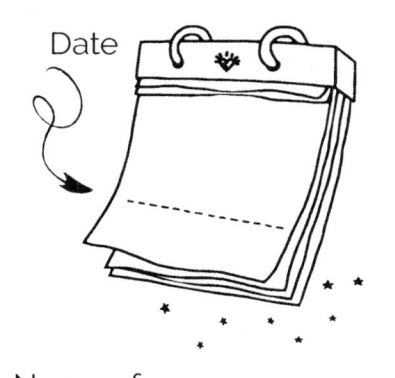

Jigsaw
EARLY YEARS CONSULTANCY

Name of room

Age of room

Ratio in room

Number of children in today	Number of children with EAL	Number of children with SEN	Number of 2 year old funded children	Number of 3 year old funded children

Staffing

Name of Staff	Qualifications	First Aid trained ✓	Safeguarding trained ✓

Date

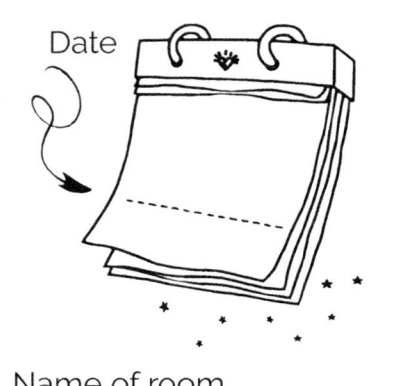

Name of room

Age of room

Ratio in room

	:

Number of children in today	Number of children with EAL	Number of children with SEN	Number of 2 year old funded children	Number of 3 year old funded children

Staffing

Name of Staff	Qualifications	First Aid trained ✓	Safeguarding trained ✓

Jigsaw
EARLY YEARS CONSULTANCY

Date

Name of room	Age of room	Ratio in room
		:

Number of children in today	Number of children with EAL	Number of children with SEN	Number of 2 year old funded children	Number of 3 year old funded children

Staffing

Name of Staff	Qualifications	First Aid trained ✓	Safeguarding trained ✓
		○	○
		○	○
		○	○
		○	○
		○	○
		○	○

Date

Name of room

Age of room

Ratio in room

:

Number of children in today

Number of children with EAL

Number of children with SEN

Number of 2 year old funded children

Number of 3 year old funded children

Staffing

Name of Staff	Qualifications	First Aid trained ✓	Safeguarding trained ✓
		○	○
		○	○
		○	○
		○	○
		○	○
		○	○

Jigsaw
EARLY YEARS CONSULTANCY

Date

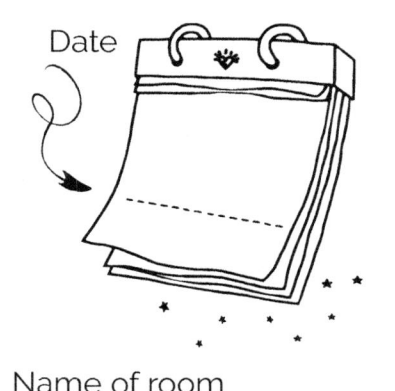

Name of room	Age of room	Ratio in room
		:

Number of children in today	Number of children with EAL	Number of children with SEN	Number of 2 year old funded children	Number of 3 year old funded children

Staffing

Name of Staff	Qualifications	First Aid trained ✓	Safeguarding trained ✓
		○	○
		○	○
		○	○
		○	○
		○	○
		○	○

Jigsaw
EARLY YEARS CONSULTANCY

Date

Name of room	Age of room	Ratio in room
		:

Number of children in today	Number of children with EAL	Number of children with SEN	Number of 2 year old funded children	Number of 3 year old funded children

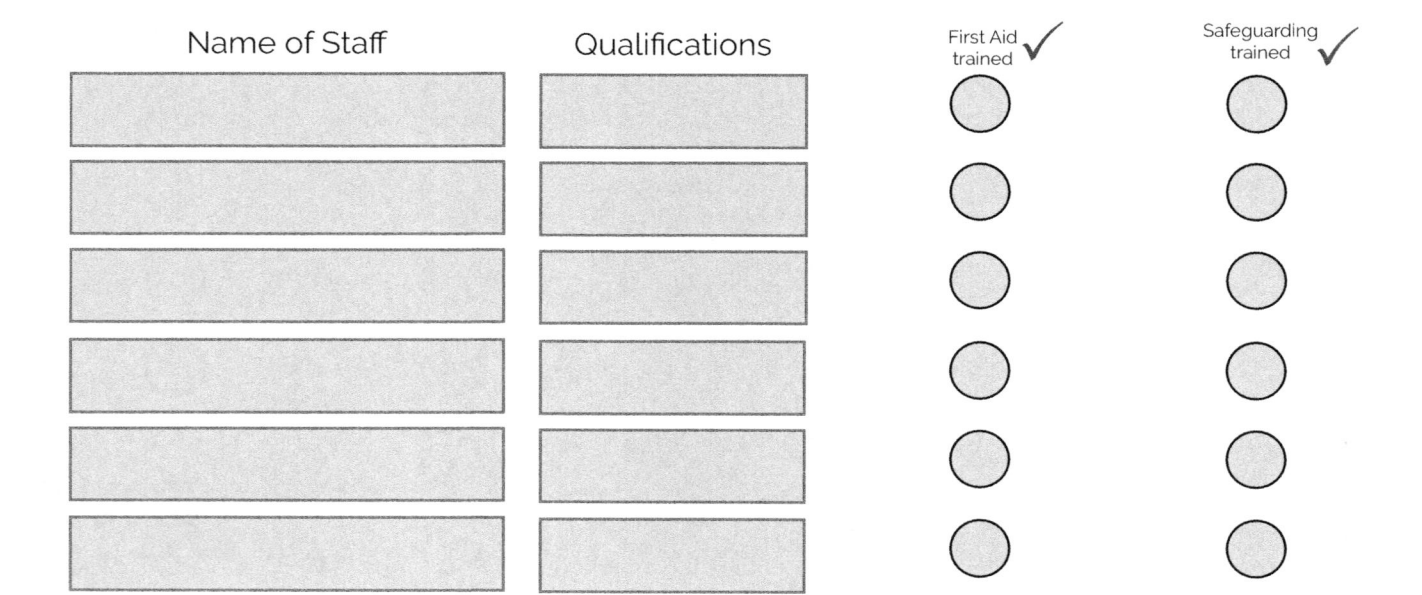

Staffing

Name of Staff	Qualifications	First Aid trained ✓	Safeguarding trained ✓
		○	○
		○	○
		○	○
		○	○
		○	○
		○	○

Jigsaw
EARLY YEARS CONSULTANCY

Date

Name of room	Age of room	Ratio in room
		:

Number of children in today	Number of children with EAL	Number of children with SEN	Number of 2 year old funded children	Number of 3 year old funded children

Staffing

Name of Staff	Qualifications	First Aid trained ✓	Safeguarding trained ✓
		◯	◯
		◯	◯
		◯	◯
		◯	◯
		◯	◯
		◯	◯

Jigsaw
EARLY YEARS CONSULTANCY

Date

Name of room	Age of room	Ratio in room
		:

Number of children in today	Number of children with EAL	Number of children with SEN	Number of 2 year old funded children	Number of 3 year old funded children

Staffing

Name of Staff	Qualifications	First Aid trained ✓	Safeguarding trained ✓
		○	○
		○	○
		○	○
		○	○
		○	○
		○	○

Date

Name of room

Age of room

Ratio in room

Number of children in today

Number of children with EAL

Number of children with SEN

Number of 2 year old funded children

Number of 3 year old funded children

Staffing

Name of Staff	Qualifications	First Aid trained ✓	Safeguarding trained ✓

Date

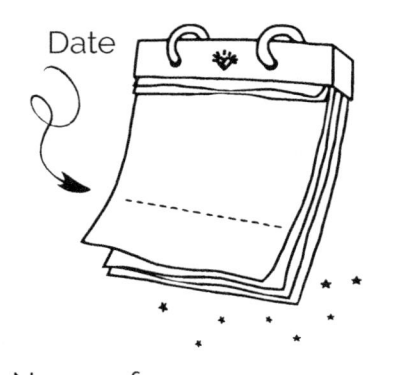

Name of room	Age of room	Ratio in room
		:

Number of children in today	Number of children with EAL	Number of children with SEN	Number of 2 year old funded children	Number of 3 year old funded children

Staffing

Name of Staff	Qualifications	First Aid trained ✓	Safeguarding trained ✓

Date

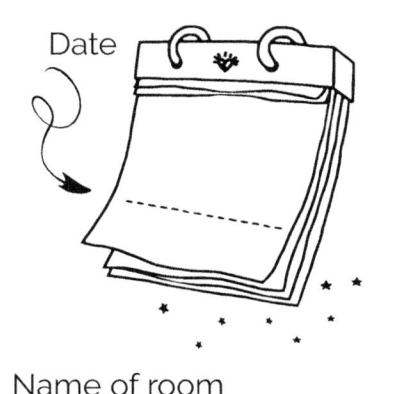

Name of room	Age of room	Ratio in room
		:

Number of children in today	Number of children with EAL	Number of children with SEN	Number of 2 year old funded children	Number of 3 year old funded children

Staffing

Name of Staff	Qualifications	First Aid trained ✓	Safeguarding trained ✓
		○	○
		○	○
		○	○
		○	○
		○	○
		○	○

Date

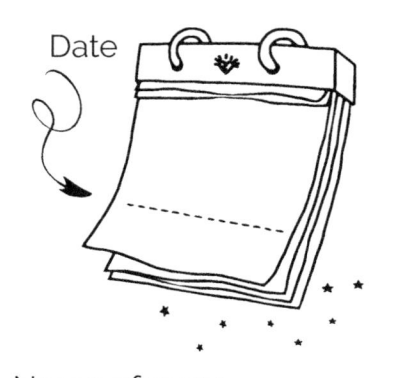

Jigsaw
EARLY YEARS CONSULTANCY

Name of room	Age of room	Ratio in room
		:

Number of children in today	Number of children with EAL	Number of children with SEN	Number of 2 year old funded children	Number of 3 year old funded children

Staffing

Name of Staff	Qualifications	First Aid trained ✓	Safeguarding trained ✓
		◯	◯
		◯	◯
		◯	◯
		◯	◯
		◯	◯
		◯	◯

Jigsaw
EARLY YEARS CONSULTANCY

Date

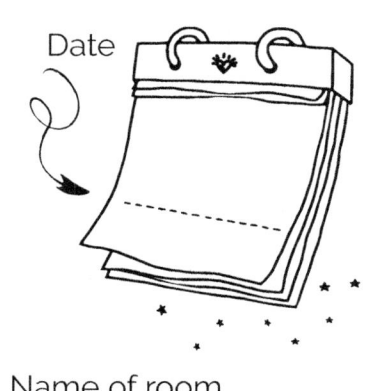

Name of room

Age of room

Ratio in room

Number of children in today	Number of children with EAL	Number of children with SEN	Number of 2 year old funded children	Number of 3 year old funded children

Staffing

Name of Staff	Qualifications	First Aid trained ✓	Safeguarding trained ✓
		○	○
		○	○
		○	○
		○	○
		○	○
		○	○

Date

Name of room	Age of room	Ratio in room
		:

Number of children in today	Number of children with EAL	Number of children with SEN	Number of 2 year old funded children	Number of 3 year old funded children

Staffing

Name of Staff	Qualifications	First Aid trained ✓	Safeguarding trained ✓
		◯	◯
		◯	◯
		◯	◯
		◯	◯
		◯	◯
		◯	◯

Jigsaw
EARLY YEARS CONSULTANCY

Date

Name of room

Age of room

Ratio in room

:

Number of children in today

Number of children with EAL

Number of children with SEN

Number of 2 year old funded children

Number of 3 year old funded children

Staffing

Name of Staff	Qualifications	First Aid trained ✓	Safeguarding trained ✓
		○	○
		○	○
		○	○
		○	○
		○	○
		○	○

Date

Name of room	Age of room	Ratio in room
		:

Number of children in today	Number of children with EAL	Number of children with SEN	Number of 2 year old funded children	Number of 3 year old funded children

Staffing

Name of Staff	Qualifications	First Aid trained ✓	Safeguarding trained ✓
		○	○
		○	○
		○	○
		○	○
		○	○
		○	○

Date

Name of room

Age of room

Ratio in room

Number of children in today	Number of children with EAL	Number of children with SEN	Number of 2 year old funded children	Number of 3 year old funded children

Staffing

Name of Staff	Qualifications	First Aid trained ✓	Safeguarding trained ✓

Jigsaw Early Years Consultancy

Date

Name of room

Age of room

Ratio in room

:

Number of children in today

Number of children with EAL

Number of children with SEN

Number of 2 year old funded children

Number of 3 year old funded children

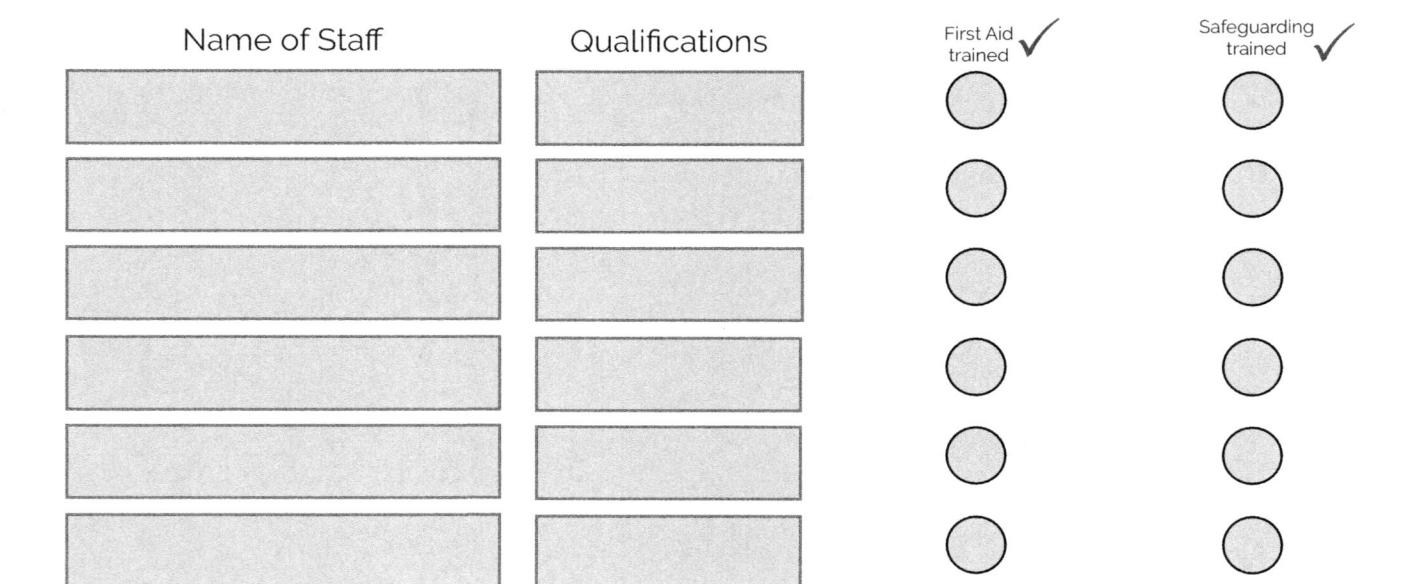

Staffing

Name of Staff	Qualifications	First Aid trained ✓	Safeguarding trained ✓
		○	○
		○	○
		○	○
		○	○
		○	○
		○	○

Jigsaw
EARLY YEARS CONSULTANCY

Date

Name of room	Age of room	Ratio in room
		:

Number of children in today	Number of children with EAL	Number of children with SEN	Number of 2 year old funded children	Number of 3 year old funded children

Staffing

Name of Staff	Qualifications	First Aid trained ✓	Safeguarding trained ✓
		◯	◯
		◯	◯
		◯	◯
		◯	◯
		◯	◯
		◯	◯

Jigsaw
EARLY YEARS CONSULTANCY

Date

Name of room	Age of room	Ratio in room
		:

Number of children in today	Number of children with EAL	Number of children with SEN	Number of 2 year old funded children	Number of 3 year old funded children

Staffing

Name of Staff	Qualifications	First Aid trained ✓	Safeguarding trained ✓
		○	○
		○	○
		○	○
		○	○
		○	○
		○	○

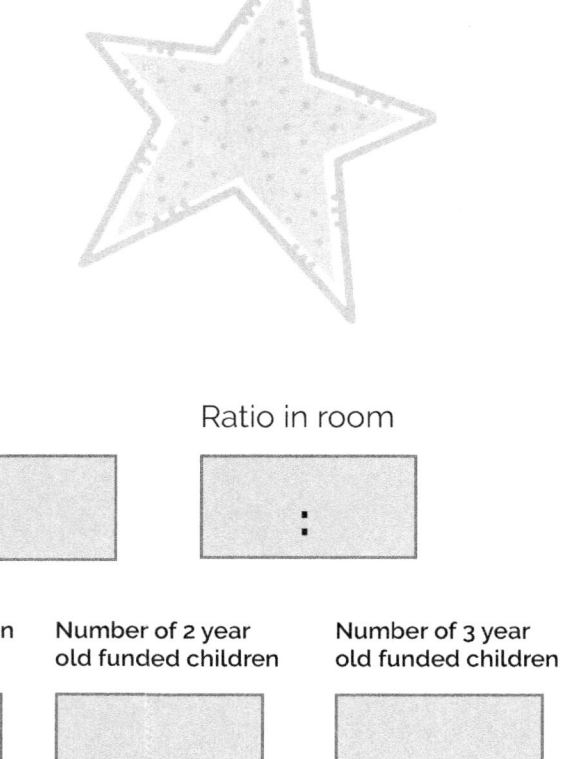

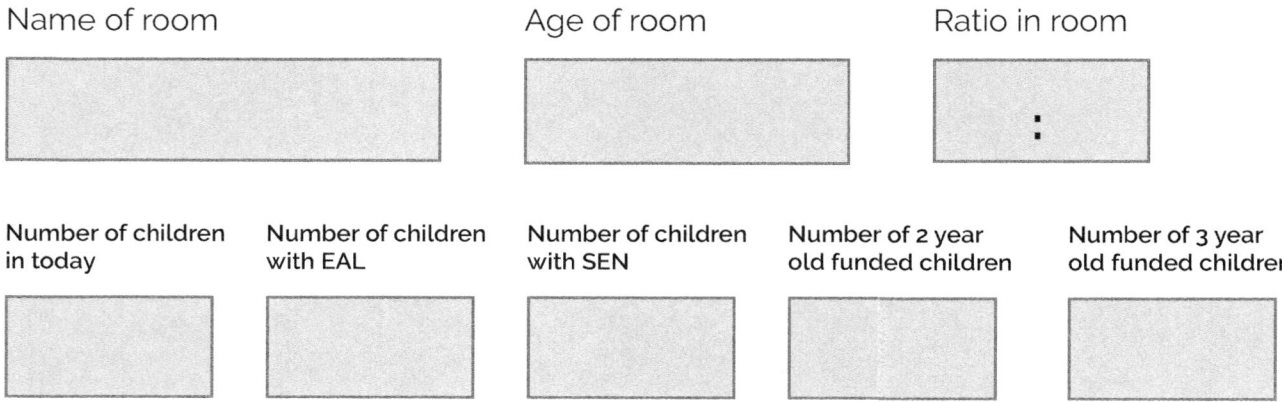

Date

Jigsaw
EARLY YEARS CONSULTANCY

Name of room	Age of room	Ratio in room
		:

Number of children in today	Number of children with EAL	Number of children with SEN	Number of 2 year old funded children	Number of 3 year old funded children

Staffing

Name of Staff	Qualifications	First Aid trained ✓	Safeguarding trained ✓
		○	○
		○	○
		○	○
		○	○
		○	○
		○	○

Date

Name of room

Age of room

Ratio in room

Number of children in today

Number of children with EAL

Number of children with SEN

Number of 2 year old funded children

Number of 3 year old funded children

Staffing

Name of Staff	Qualifications	First Aid trained ✓	Safeguarding trained ✓

Jigsaw
EARLY YEARS CONSULTANCY

Date

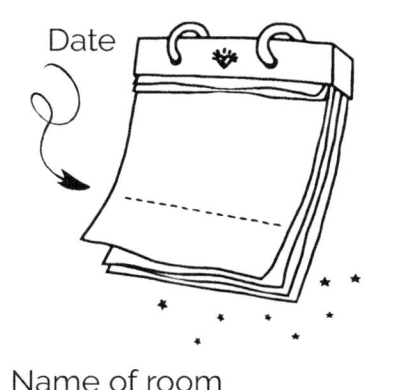

Name of room

Age of room

Ratio in room

Number of children in today	Number of children with EAL	Number of children with SEN	Number of 2 year old funded children	Number of 3 year old funded children

Staffing

Name of Staff	Qualifications	First Aid trained ✓	Safeguarding trained ✓
		○	○
		○	○
		○	○
		○	○
		○	○
		○	○

Date

Name of room

Age of room

Ratio in room

:

Number of children in today	Number of children with EAL	Number of children with SEN	Number of 2 year old funded children	Number of 3 year old funded children

Staffing

Name of Staff	Qualifications	First Aid trained ✓	Safeguarding trained ✓
		○	○
		○	○
		○	○
		○	○
		○	○
		○	○

Jigsaw
EARLY YEARS CONSULTANCY

Date

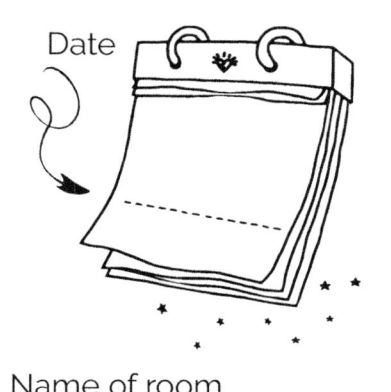

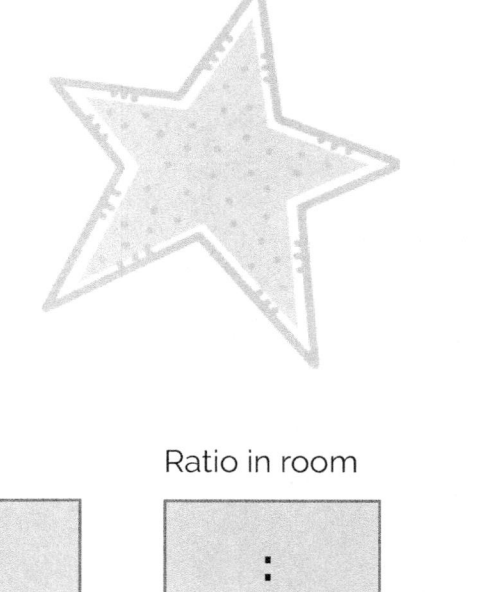

Name of room

Age of room

Ratio in room

:

Number of children in today

Number of children with EAL

Number of children with SEN

Number of 2 year old funded children

Number of 3 year old funded children

Staffing

Name of Staff	Qualifications	First Aid trained ✓	Safeguarding trained ✓
		◯	◯
		◯	◯
		◯	◯
		◯	◯
		◯	◯
		◯	◯

Jigsaw
EARLY YEARS CONSULTANCY

Date

Name of room

Age of room

Ratio in room

| | : | |

Number of children in today

Number of children with EAL

Number of children with SEN

Number of 2 year old funded children

Number of 3 year old funded children

Staffing

Name of Staff	Qualifications	First Aid trained ✓	Safeguarding trained ✓
		○	○
		○	○
		○	○
		○	○
		○	○
		○	○

Jigsaw
EARLY YEARS CONSULTANCY

Date

Name of room	Age of room	Ratio in room
		:

Number of children in today	Number of children with EAL	Number of children with SEN	Number of 2 year old funded children	Number of 3 year old funded children

Staffing

Name of Staff	Qualifications	First Aid trained ✓	Safeguarding trained ✓
		○	○
		○	○
		○	○
		○	○
		○	○
		○	○

Jigsaw
EARLY YEARS CONSULTANCY

Date

Name of room	Age of room	Ratio in room
		:

Number of children in today	Number of children with EAL	Number of children with SEN	Number of 2 year old funded children	Number of 3 year old funded children

Staffing

Name of Staff	Qualifications	First Aid trained ✓	Safeguarding trained ✓
		○	○
		○	○
		○	○
		○	○
		○	○
		○	○

Date

Name of room

Age of room

Ratio in room

Number of children in today	Number of children with EAL	Number of children with SEN	Number of 2 year old funded children	Number of 3 year old funded children

Staffing

Name of Staff	Qualifications	First Aid trained ✓	Safeguarding trained ✓
		○	○
		○	○
		○	○
		○	○
		○	○
		○	○

Jigsaw Early Years Consultancy

Date

Name of room	Age of room	Ratio in room
		:

Number of children in today	Number of children with EAL	Number of children with SEN	Number of 2 year old funded children	Number of 3 year old funded children

Staffing

Name of Staff	Qualifications	First Aid trained ✓	Safeguarding trained ✓
		○	○
		○	○
		○	○
		○	○
		○	○
		○	○

Date

Name of room

Age of room

Ratio in room

Number of children in today

Number of children with EAL

Number of children with SEN

Number of 2 year old funded children

Number of 3 year old funded children

Staffing

Name of Staff	Qualifications	First Aid trained ✓	Safeguarding trained ✓

Jigsaw
EARLY YEARS CONSULTANCY

Date

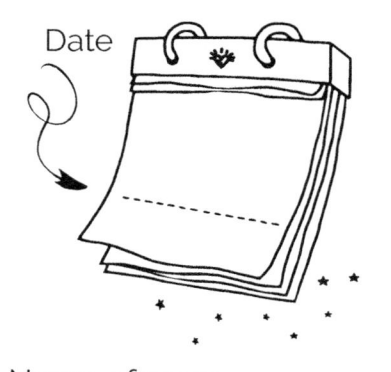

Name of room	Age of room	Ratio in room
		:

Number of children in today	Number of children with EAL	Number of children with SEN	Number of 2 year old funded children	Number of 3 year old funded children

Staffing

Name of Staff	Qualifications	First Aid trained ✓	Safeguarding trained ✓
		○	○
		○	○
		○	○
		○	○
		○	○
		○	○

Date

Name of room

Age of room

Ratio in room

Number of children in today	Number of children with EAL	Number of children with SEN	Number of 2 year old funded children	Number of 3 year old funded children

Staffing

Name of Staff	Qualifications	First Aid trained ✓	Safeguarding trained ✓

Jigsaw
EARLY YEARS CONSULTANCY

Date

Name of room	Age of room	Ratio in room
		:

Number of children in today	Number of children with EAL	Number of children with SEN	Number of 2 year old funded children	Number of 3 year old funded children

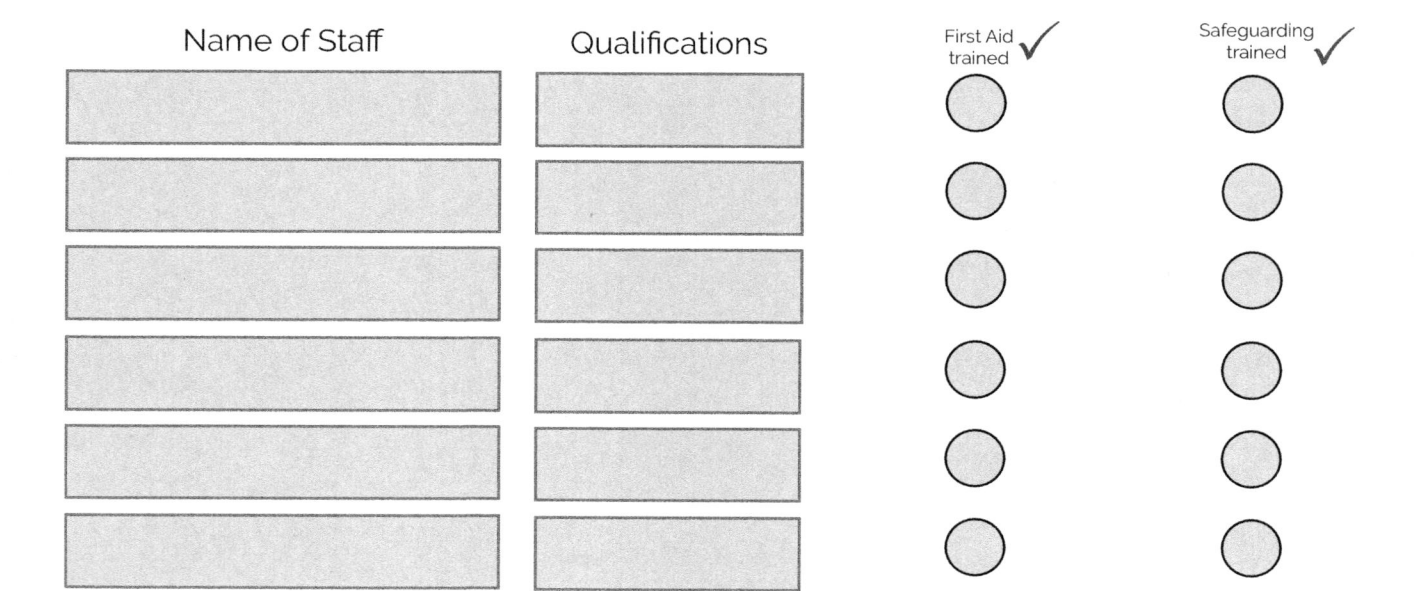

Staffing

Name of Staff	Qualifications	First Aid trained ✓	Safeguarding trained ✓
		○	○
		○	○
		○	○
		○	○
		○	○
		○	○

Jigsaw
EARLY YEARS CONSULTANCY

Date

Name of room	Age of room	Ratio in room
		:

Number of children in today	Number of children with EAL	Number of children with SEN	Number of 2 year old funded children	Number of 3 year old funded children

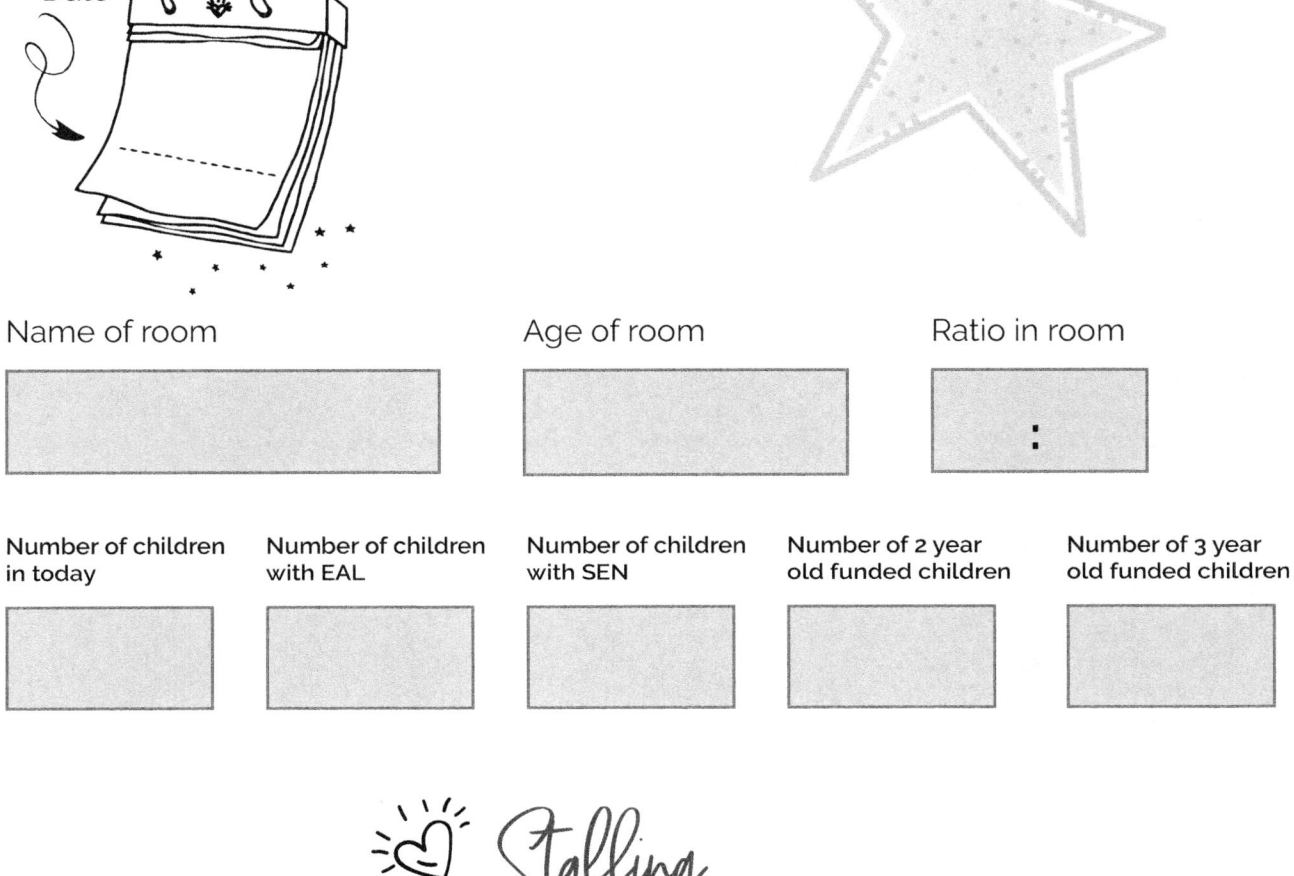

Staffing

Name of Staff	Qualifications	First Aid trained ✓	Safeguarding trained ✓
		○	○
		○	○
		○	○
		○	○
		○	○
		○	○

Date

Jigsaw
EARLY YEARS CONSULTANCY

Name of room	Age of room	Ratio in room
		:

Number of children in today	Number of children with EAL	Number of children with SEN	Number of 2 year old funded children	Number of 3 year old funded children

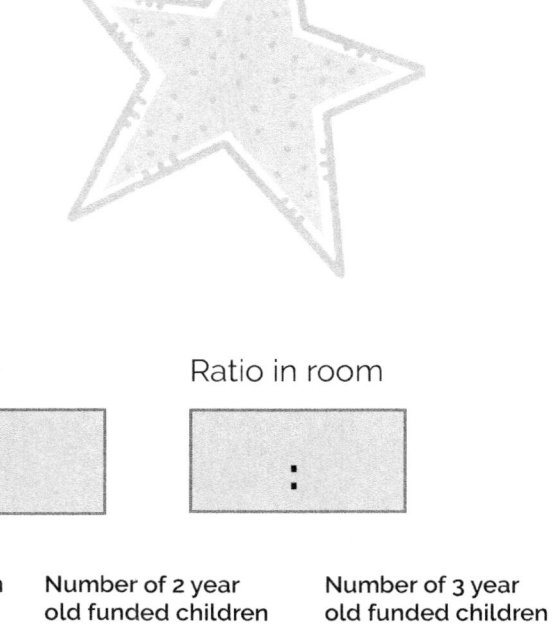

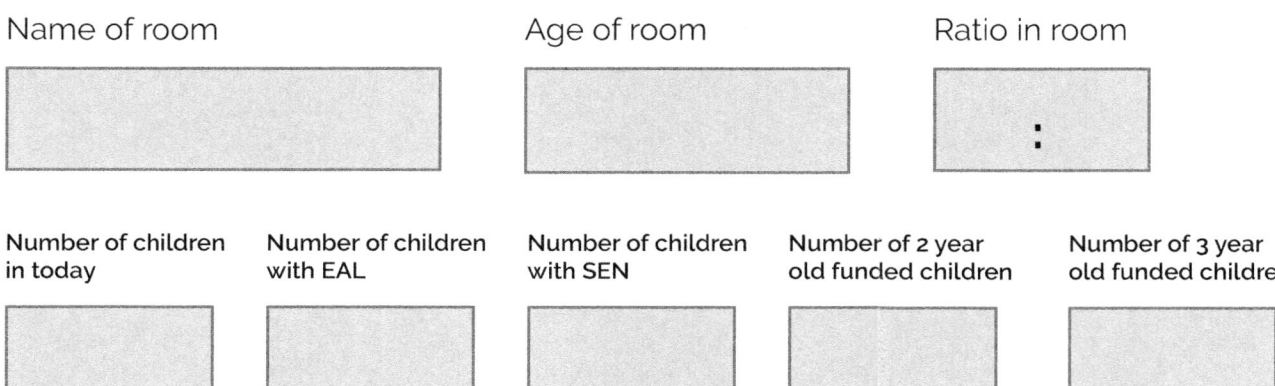

Staffing

Name of Staff	Qualifications	First Aid trained ✓	Safeguarding trained ✓

Date

Jigsaw
EARLY YEARS CONSULTANCY

Name of room	Age of room	Ratio in room
		:

Number of children in today	Number of children with EAL	Number of children with SEN	Number of 2 year old funded children	Number of 3 year old funded children

Staffing

Name of Staff	Qualifications	First Aid trained ✓	Safeguarding trained ✓
		○	○
		○	○
		○	○
		○	○
		○	○
		○	○

Date

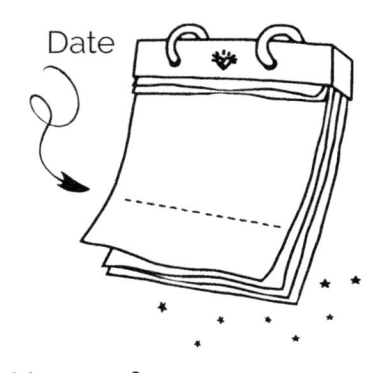

Name of room

Age of room

Ratio in room

:

Number of children in today

Number of children with EAL

Number of children with SEN

Number of 2 year old funded children

Number of 3 year old funded children

Staffing

Name of Staff	Qualifications	First Aid trained ✓	Safeguarding trained ✓
		○	○
		○	○
		○	○
		○	○
		○	○
		○	○

Jigsaw
EARLY YEARS CONSULTANCY

Date

Name of room	Age of room	Ratio in room
		:

Number of children in today	Number of children with EAL	Number of children with SEN	Number of 2 year old funded children	Number of 3 year old funded children

Staffing

Name of Staff	Qualifications	First Aid trained ✓	Safeguarding trained ✓
		○	○
		○	○
		○	○
		○	○
		○	○
		○	○

Date

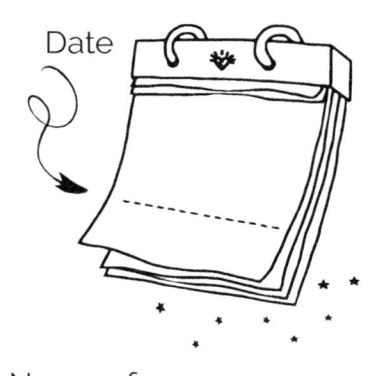

Name of room	Age of room	Ratio in room
		:

Number of children in today	Number of children with EAL	Number of children with SEN	Number of 2 year old funded children	Number of 3 year old funded children

Staffing

Name of Staff	Qualifications	First Aid trained ✓	Safeguarding trained ✓
		○	○
		○	○
		○	○
		○	○
		○	○
		○	○

Date

Name of room

Age of room

Ratio in room

:

Number of children in today

Number of children with EAL

Number of children with SEN

Number of 2 year old funded children

Number of 3 year old funded children

Staffing

Name of Staff	Qualifications	First Aid trained ✓	Safeguarding trained ✓

Date

Name of room

Age of room

Ratio in room

:

Number of children in today

Number of children with EAL

Number of children with SEN

Number of 2 year old funded children

Number of 3 year old funded children

Staffing

Name of Staff	Qualifications	First Aid trained ✓	Safeguarding trained ✓
		◯	◯
		◯	◯
		◯	◯
		◯	◯
		◯	◯
		◯	◯

Date

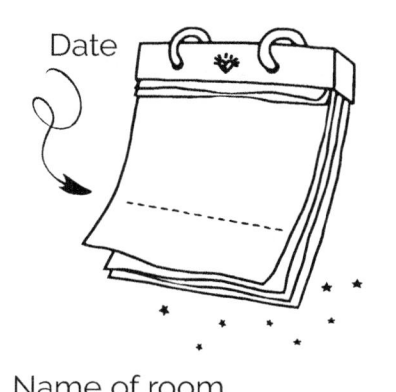

Name of room

Age of room

Ratio in room

:

Number of children in today

Number of children with EAL

Number of children with SEN

Number of 2 year old funded children

Number of 3 year old funded children

Staffing

Name of Staff	Qualifications	First Aid trained ✓	Safeguarding trained ✓

Date

Jigsaw
EARLY YEARS CONSULTANCY

Name of room

Age of room

Ratio in room

:

Number of children in today

Number of children with EAL

Number of children with SEN

Number of 2 year old funded children

Number of 3 year old funded children

Staffing

Name of Staff	Qualifications	First Aid trained ✓	Safeguarding trained ✓
		◯	◯
		◯	◯
		◯	◯
		◯	◯
		◯	◯
		◯	◯

Date

Name of room

Age of room

Ratio in room

:

Number of children in today

Number of children with EAL

Number of children with SEN

Number of 2 year old funded children

Number of 3 year old funded children

Staffing

Name of Staff	Qualifications	First Aid trained ✓	Safeguarding trained ✓

Jigsaw
EARLY YEARS CONSULTANCY

Date

Name of room	Age of room	Ratio in room
		:

Number of children in today	Number of children with EAL	Number of children with SEN	Number of 2 year old funded children	Number of 3 year old funded children

Staffing

Name of Staff	Qualifications	First Aid trained ✓	Safeguarding trained ✓

Date

Name of room

Age of room

Ratio in room

:

Number of children in today	Number of children with EAL	Number of children with SEN	Number of 2 year old funded children	Number of 3 year old funded children

Staffing

Name of Staff	Qualifications	First Aid trained ✓	Safeguarding trained ✓

Date

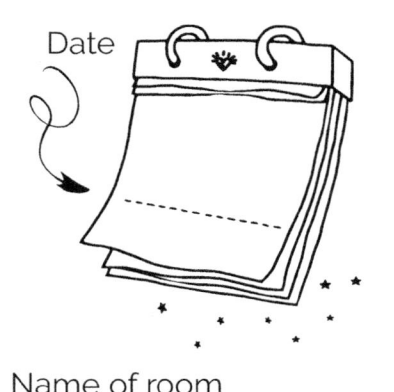

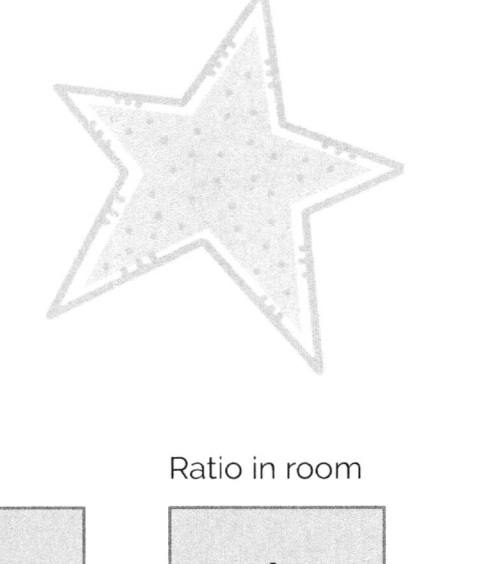

Name of room	Age of room	Ratio in room
		:

Number of children in today	Number of children with EAL	Number of children with SEN	Number of 2 year old funded children	Number of 3 year old funded children

Staffing

Name of Staff	Qualifications	First Aid trained ✓	Safeguarding trained ✓
		◯	◯
		◯	◯
		◯	◯
		◯	◯
		◯	◯
		◯	◯

Jigsaw
EARLY YEARS CONSULTANCY

Date

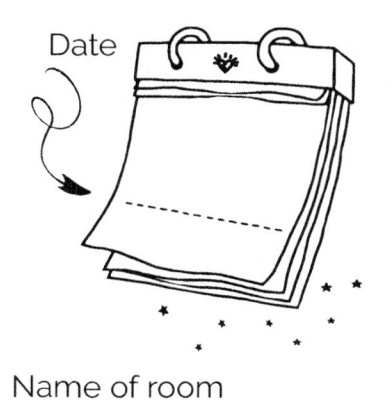

Name of room

Age of room

Ratio in room

:

Number of children in today

Number of children with EAL

Number of children with SEN

Number of 2 year old funded children

Number of 3 year old funded children

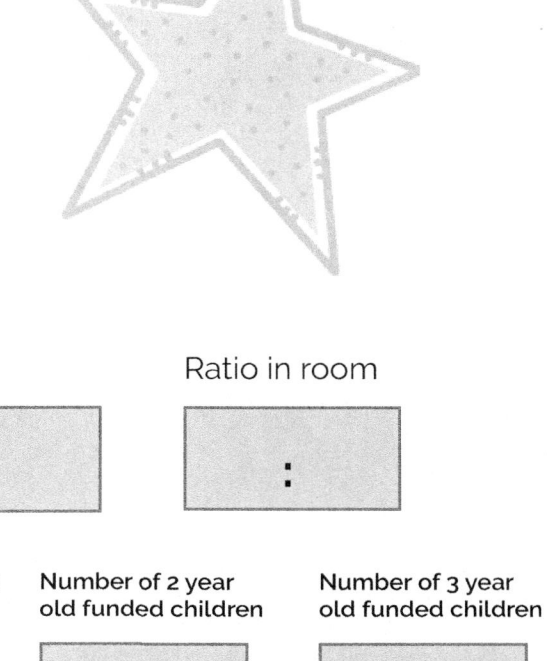

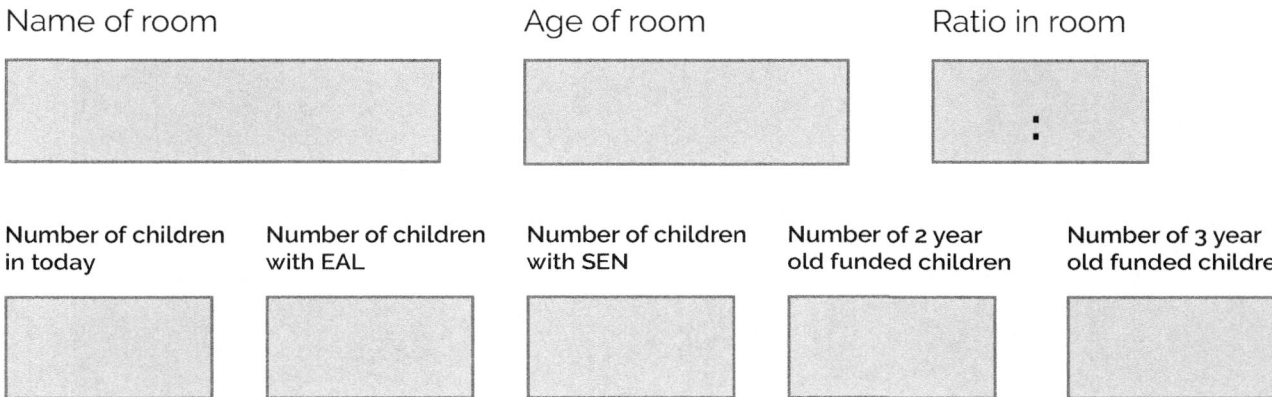

Staffing

Name of Staff	Qualifications	First Aid trained ✓	Safeguarding trained ✓
		◯	◯
		◯	◯
		◯	◯
		◯	◯
		◯	◯
		◯	◯

Date

Name of room

Age of room

Ratio in room

:

Number of children in today	Number of children with EAL	Number of children with SEN	Number of 2 year old funded children	Number of 3 year old funded children

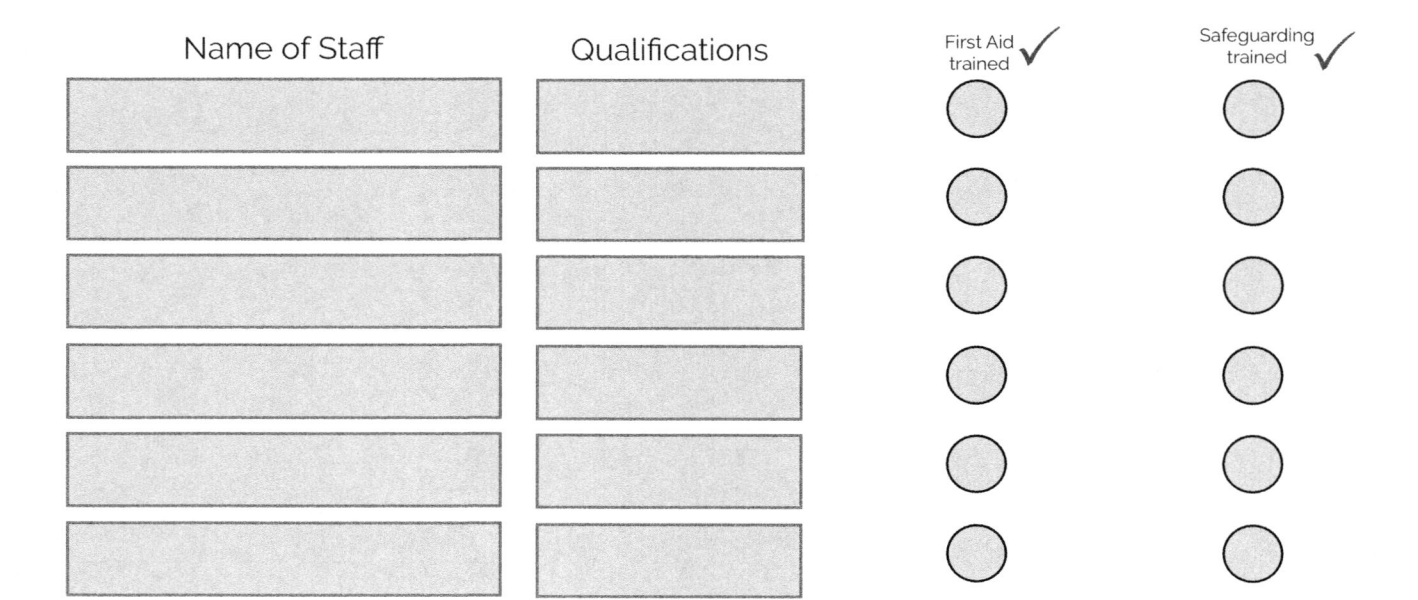

Staffing

Name of Staff	Qualifications	First Aid trained ✓	Safeguarding trained ✓
		○	○
		○	○
		○	○
		○	○
		○	○
		○	○

Date

Name of room

Age of room

Ratio in room

Number of children in today

Number of children with EAL

Number of children with SEN

Number of 2 year old funded children

Number of 3 year old funded children

Staffing

Name of Staff	Qualifications	First Aid trained ✓	Safeguarding trained ✓

Date

Jigsaw
EARLY YEARS CONSULTANCY

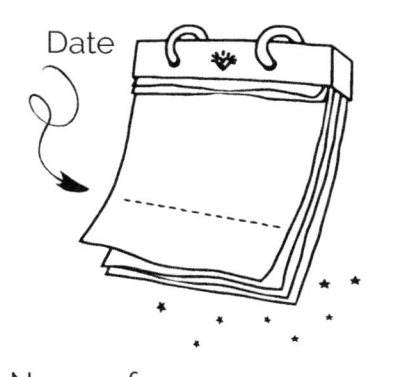

Name of room	Age of room	Ratio in room
		:

Number of children in today	Number of children with EAL	Number of children with SEN	Number of 2 year old funded children	Number of 3 year old funded children

Staffing

Name of Staff	Qualifications	First Aid trained ✓	Safeguarding trained ✓
		◯	◯
		◯	◯
		◯	◯
		◯	◯
		◯	◯
		◯	◯

Date

Name of room

Age of room

Ratio in room

Number of children in today	Number of children with EAL	Number of children with SEN	Number of 2 year old funded children	Number of 3 year old funded children

Staffing

Name of Staff	Qualifications	First Aid trained ✓	Safeguarding trained ✓

Date

Name of room

Age of room

Ratio in room

:

Number of children in today

Number of children with EAL

Number of children with SEN

Number of 2 year old funded children

Number of 3 year old funded children

Staffing

Name of Staff	Qualifications	First Aid trained ✓	Safeguarding trained ✓
		○	○
		○	○
		○	○
		○	○
		○	○
		○	○

Date

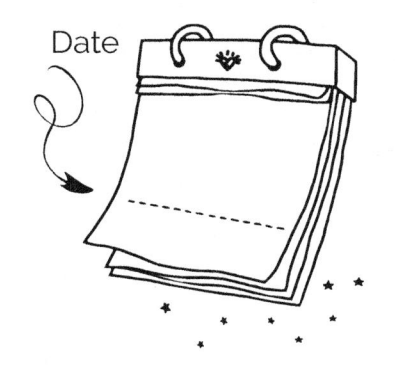

Name of room	Age of room	Ratio in room
		:

Number of children in today	Number of children with EAL	Number of children with SEN	Number of 2 year old funded children	Number of 3 year old funded children

Staffing

Name of Staff	Qualifications	First Aid trained ✓	Safeguarding trained ✓
		○	○
		○	○
		○	○
		○	○
		○	○
		○	○

Date

Name of room

Age of room

Ratio in room

Number of children in today

Number of children with EAL

Number of children with SEN

Number of 2 year old funded children

Number of 3 year old funded children

Staffing

Name of Staff	Qualifications	First Aid trained ✓	Safeguarding trained ✓
		○	○
		○	○
		○	○
		○	○
		○	○
		○	○

Date

Name of room

Age of room

Ratio in room

:

Number of children in today

Number of children with EAL

Number of children with SEN

Number of 2 year old funded children

Number of 3 year old funded children

Staffing

Name of Staff	Qualifications	First Aid trained ✓	Safeguarding trained ✓
		○	○
		○	○
		○	○
		○	○
		○	○
		○	○

Jigsaw Early Years Consultancy

Date

Name of room	Age of room	Ratio in room
		:

Number of children in today	Number of children with EAL	Number of children with SEN	Number of 2 year old funded children	Number of 3 year old funded children

Staffing

Name of Staff	Qualifications	First Aid trained ✓	Safeguarding trained ✓
		○	○
		○	○
		○	○
		○	○
		○	○
		○	○

Date

Name of room

Age of room

Ratio in room

Number of children in today	Number of children with EAL	Number of children with SEN	Number of 2 year old funded children	Number of 3 year old funded children

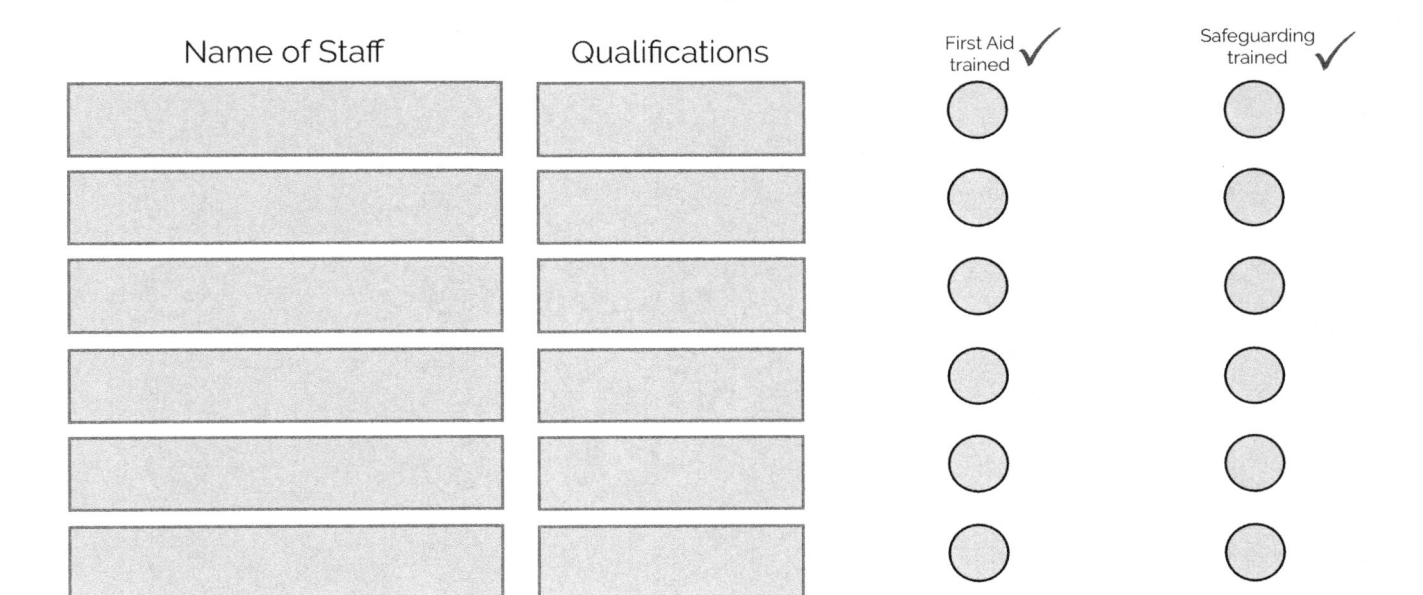

Staffing

Name of Staff	Qualifications	First Aid trained ✓	Safeguarding trained ✓

Date

Name of room

Age of room

Ratio in room

Number of children in today

Number of children with EAL

Number of children with SEN

Number of 2 year old funded children

Number of 3 year old funded children

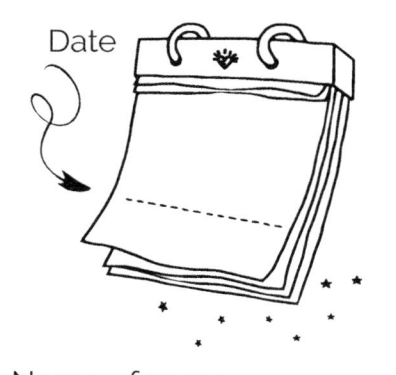

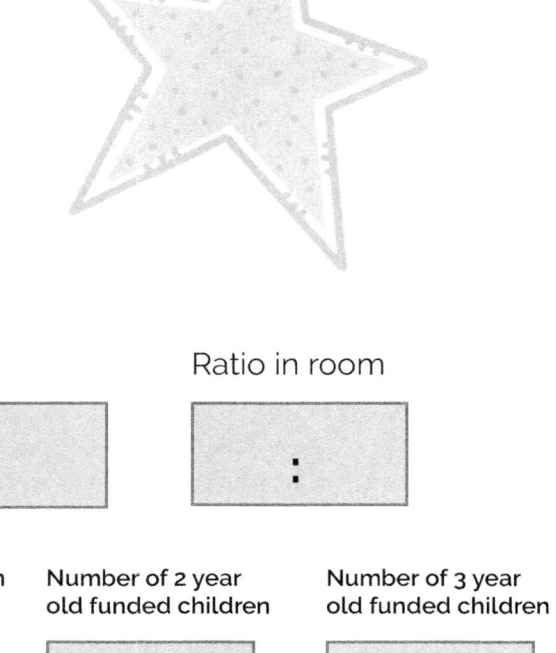

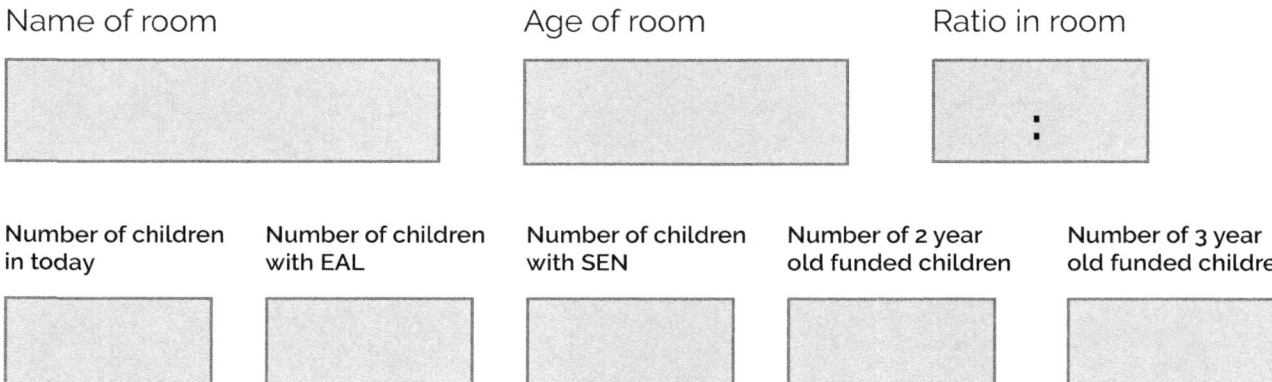

Staffing

Name of Staff	Qualifications	First Aid trained ✓	Safeguarding trained ✓
		○	○
		○	○
		○	○
		○	○
		○	○
		○	○

Jigsaw
EARLY YEARS CONSULTANCY

Date

Name of room	Age of room	Ratio in room
		:

Number of children in today	Number of children with EAL	Number of children with SEN	Number of 2 year old funded children	Number of 3 year old funded children

Staffing

Name of Staff	Qualifications	First Aid trained ✓	Safeguarding trained ✓
		○	○
		○	○
		○	○
		○	○
		○	○
		○	○

Date

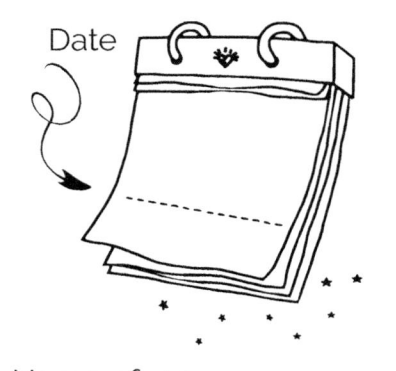

Name of room

Age of room

Ratio in room

:

Number of children in today

Number of children with EAL

Number of children with SEN

Number of 2 year old funded children

Number of 3 year old funded children

Staffing

Name of Staff	Qualifications	First Aid trained ✓	Safeguarding trained ✓
		○	○
		○	○
		○	○
		○	○
		○	○
		○	○

Date

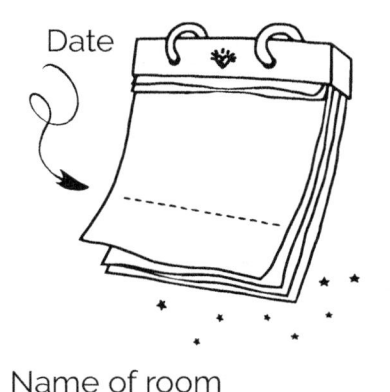

Name of room	Age of room	Ratio in room
		:

Number of children in today	Number of children with EAL	Number of children with SEN	Number of 2 year old funded children	Number of 3 year old funded children

Staffing

Name of Staff	Qualifications	First Aid trained ✓	Safeguarding trained ✓

Date

Name of room	Age of room	Ratio in room
		:

Number of children in today	Number of children with EAL	Number of children with SEN	Number of 2 year old funded children	Number of 3 year old funded children

Staffing

Name of Staff	Qualifications	First Aid trained ✓	Safeguarding trained ✓
		○	○
		○	○
		○	○
		○	○
		○	○
		○	○

Jigsaw
EARLY YEARS CONSULTANCY

Date

Name of room

Age of room

Ratio in room

Number of children in today

Number of children with EAL

Number of children with SEN

Number of 2 year old funded children

Number of 3 year old funded children

Staffing

Name of Staff	Qualifications	First Aid trained ✓	Safeguarding trained ✓

Date

Name of room

Age of room

Ratio in room

:

Number of children in today	Number of children with EAL	Number of children with SEN	Number of 2 year old funded children	Number of 3 year old funded children

Staffing

Name of Staff	Qualifications	First Aid trained ✓	Safeguarding trained ✓
		◯	◯
		◯	◯
		◯	◯
		◯	◯
		◯	◯
		◯	◯

Date

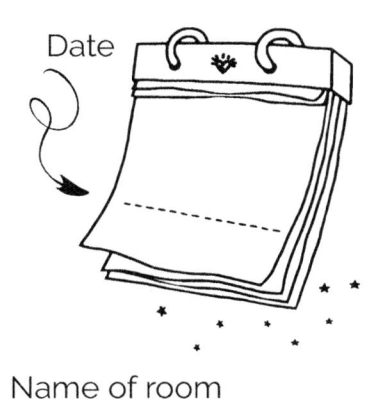

Name of room	Age of room	Ratio in room
		:

Number of children in today	Number of children with EAL	Number of children with SEN	Number of 2 year old funded children	Number of 3 year old funded children

Staffing

Name of Staff	Qualifications	First Aid trained ✓	Safeguarding trained ✓
		◯	◯
		◯	◯
		◯	◯
		◯	◯
		◯	◯
		◯	◯

Jigsaw
EARLY YEARS CONSULTANCY

Date

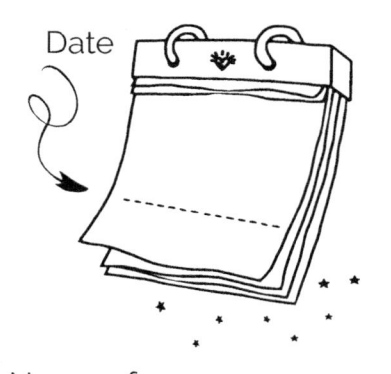

Name of room	Age of room	Ratio in room
		:

Number of children in today	Number of children with EAL	Number of children with SEN	Number of 2 year old funded children	Number of 3 year old funded children

Staffing

Name of Staff	Qualifications	First Aid trained ✓	Safeguarding trained ✓
		○	○
		○	○
		○	○
		○	○
		○	○
		○	○

Jigsaw
EARLY YEARS CONSULTANCY

Date

Name of room

Age of room

Ratio in room

:

Number of children in today

Number of children with EAL

Number of children with SEN

Number of 2 year old funded children

Number of 3 year old funded children

Staffing

Name of Staff	Qualifications	First Aid trained ✓	Safeguarding trained ✓
		○	○
		○	○
		○	○
		○	○
		○	○
		○	○

Date

Jigsaw
EARLY YEARS CONSULTANCY

Name of room	Age of room	Ratio in room
		:

Number of children in today	Number of children with EAL	Number of children with SEN	Number of 2 year old funded children	Number of 3 year old funded children

Staffing

Name of Staff	Qualifications	First Aid trained ✓	Safeguarding trained ✓
		○	○
		○	○
		○	○
		○	○
		○	○
		○	○

Jigsaw
EARLY YEARS CONSULTANCY

Date

Name of room	Age of room	Ratio in room
		:

Number of children in today	Number of children with EAL	Number of children with SEN	Number of 2 year old funded children	Number of 3 year old funded children

Staffing

Name of Staff	Qualifications	First Aid trained ✓	Safeguarding trained ✓
		◯	◯
		◯	◯
		◯	◯
		◯	◯
		◯	◯
		◯	◯

Date

Name of room	Age of room	Ratio in room
		:

Number of children in today	Number of children with EAL	Number of children with SEN	Number of 2 year old funded children	Number of 3 year old funded children

Staffing

Name of Staff	Qualifications	First Aid trained ✓	Safeguarding trained ✓
		◯	◯
		◯	◯
		◯	◯
		◯	◯
		◯	◯
		◯	◯

Jigsaw
EARLY YEARS CONSULTANCY

Date

Name of room	Age of room	Ratio in room
		:

Number of children in today	Number of children with EAL	Number of children with SEN	Number of 2 year old funded children	Number of 3 year old funded children

Staffing

Name of Staff	Qualifications	First Aid trained ✓	Safeguarding trained ✓
		○	○
		○	○
		○	○
		○	○
		○	○
		○	○

Jigsaw Early Years Consultancy

Date

Name of room	Age of room	Ratio in room
		:

Number of children in today	Number of children with EAL	Number of children with SEN	Number of 2 year old funded children	Number of 3 year old funded children

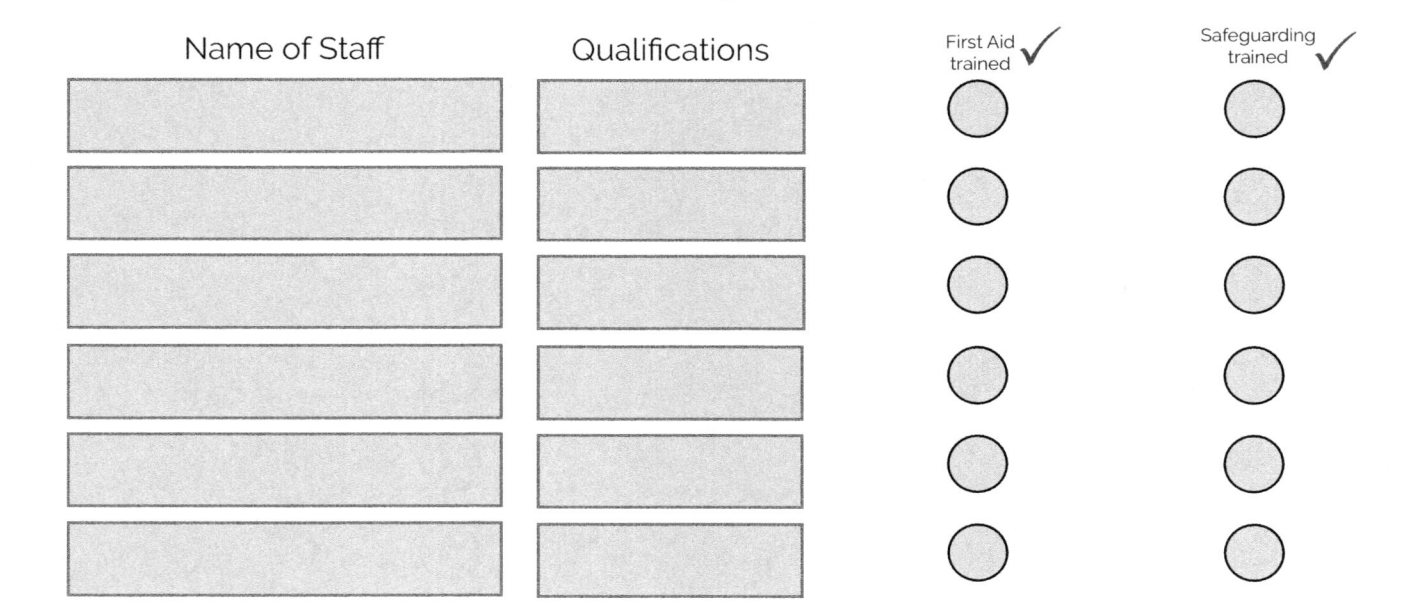

Staffing

Name of Staff	Qualifications	First Aid trained ✓	Safeguarding trained ✓
		○	○
		○	○
		○	○
		○	○
		○	○
		○	○

Jigsaw
EARLY YEARS CONSULTANCY

Date

Name of room

Age of room

Ratio in room
:

Number of children in today

Number of children with EAL

Number of children with SEN

Number of 2 year old funded children

Number of 3 year old funded children

Staffing

Name of Staff	Qualifications	First Aid trained ✓	Safeguarding trained ✓
		○	○
		○	○
		○	○
		○	○
		○	○
		○	○

Jigsaw Early Years Consultancy

Date

Name of room	Age of room	Ratio in room
		:

Number of children in today	Number of children with EAL	Number of children with SEN	Number of 2 year old funded children	Number of 3 year old funded children

Staffing

Name of Staff	Qualifications	First Aid trained ✓	Safeguarding trained ✓
		○	○
		○	○
		○	○
		○	○
		○	○
		○	○

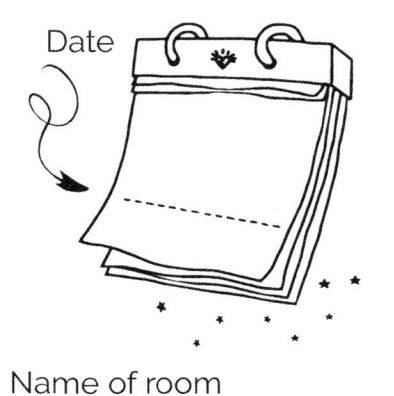

Date

Jigsaw
EARLY YEARS CONSULTANCY

Name of room

Age of room

Ratio in room

| Number of children in today | Number of children with EAL | Number of children with SEN | Number of 2 year old funded children | Number of 3 year old funded children |

Staffing

Name of Staff	Qualifications	First Aid trained ✓	Safeguarding trained ✓

Date

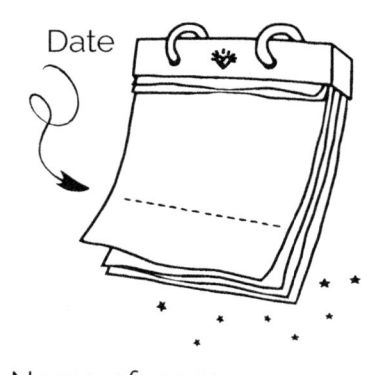

Name of room	Age of room	Ratio in room
		:

Number of children in today	Number of children with EAL	Number of children with SEN	Number of 2 year old funded children	Number of 3 year old funded children

Staffing

Name of Staff	Qualifications	First Aid trained ✓	Safeguarding trained ✓
		○	○
		○	○
		○	○
		○	○
		○	○
		○	○

Date

Name of room	Age of room	Ratio in room
		:

Number of children in today	Number of children with EAL	Number of children with SEN	Number of 2 year old funded children	Number of 3 year old funded children

Staffing

Name of Staff	Qualifications	First Aid trained ✓	Safeguarding trained ✓
		○	○
		○	○
		○	○
		○	○
		○	○
		○	○

Date

Name of room

Age of room

Ratio in room

| | | : |

Number of children in today

Number of children with EAL

Number of children with SEN

Number of 2 year old funded children

Number of 3 year old funded children

Staffing

Name of Staff	Qualifications	First Aid trained ✓	Safeguarding trained ✓
		◯	◯
		◯	◯
		◯	◯
		◯	◯
		◯	◯
		◯	◯

Jigsaw
EARLY YEARS CONSULTANCY

Date

Name of room	Age of room	Ratio in room
		:

Number of children in today	Number of children with EAL	Number of children with SEN	Number of 2 year old funded children	Number of 3 year old funded children

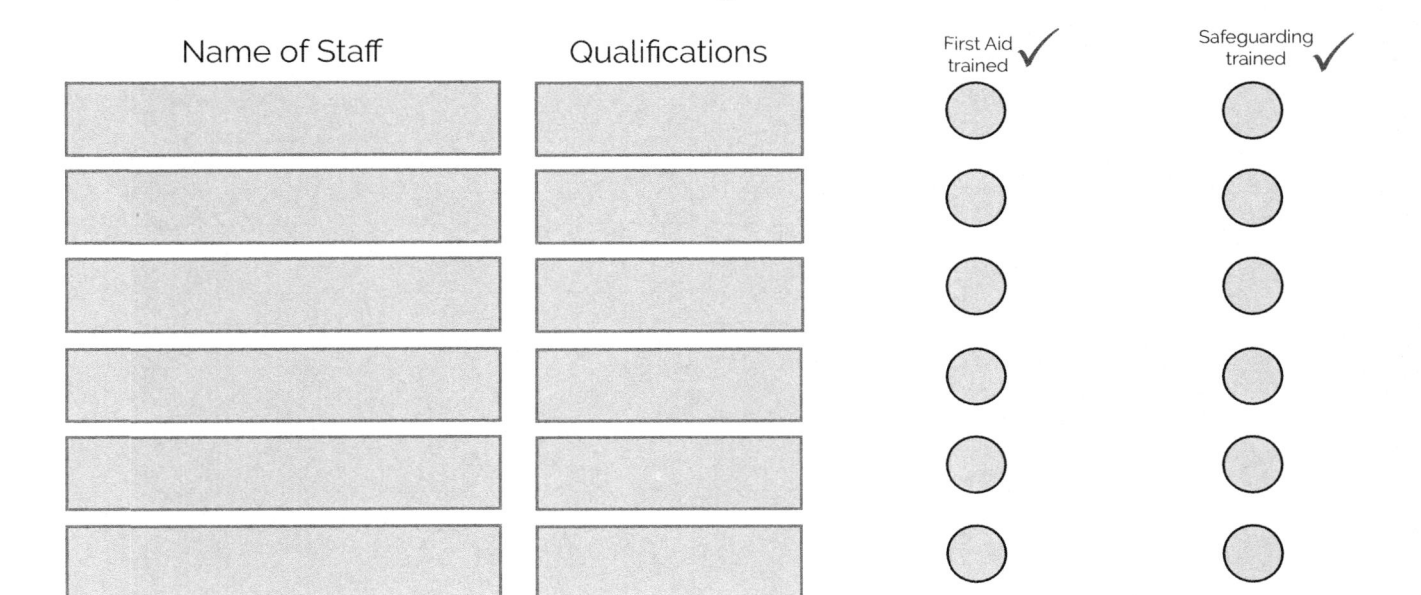

Staffing

Name of Staff	Qualifications	First Aid trained ✓	Safeguarding trained ✓
		○	○
		○	○
		○	○
		○	○
		○	○
		○	○

Date

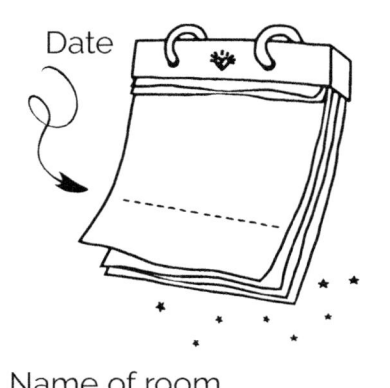

Name of room	Age of room	Ratio in room
		:

Number of children in today	Number of children with EAL	Number of children with SEN	Number of 2 year old funded children	Number of 3 year old funded children

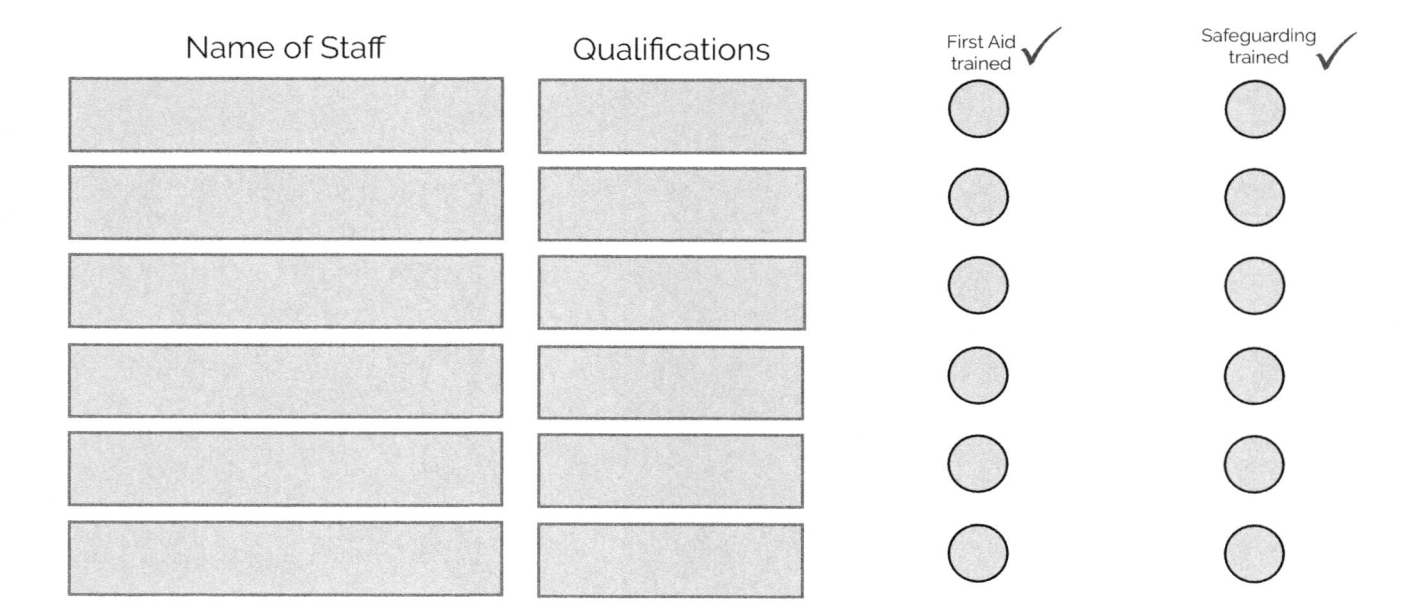

Staffing

Name of Staff	Qualifications	First Aid trained ✓	Safeguarding trained ✓
		○	○
		○	○
		○	○
		○	○
		○	○
		○	○

Jigsaw
EARLY YEARS CONSULTANCY

Date

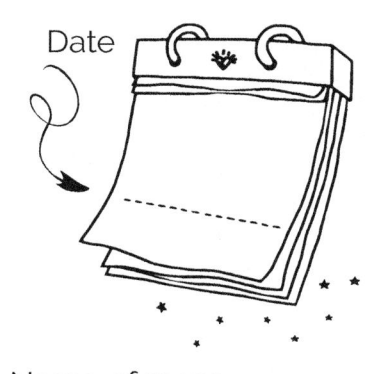

Name of room	Age of room	Ratio in room
		:

Number of children in today	Number of children with EAL	Number of children with SEN	Number of 2 year old funded children	Number of 3 year old funded children

Staffing

Name of Staff	Qualifications	First Aid trained ✓	Safeguarding trained ✓
		◯	◯
		◯	◯
		◯	◯
		◯	◯
		◯	◯
		◯	◯

Jigsaw
EARLY YEARS CONSULTANCY

Date

Name of room	Age of room	Ratio in room
		:

Number of children in today	Number of children with EAL	Number of children with SEN	Number of 2 year old funded children	Number of 3 year old funded children

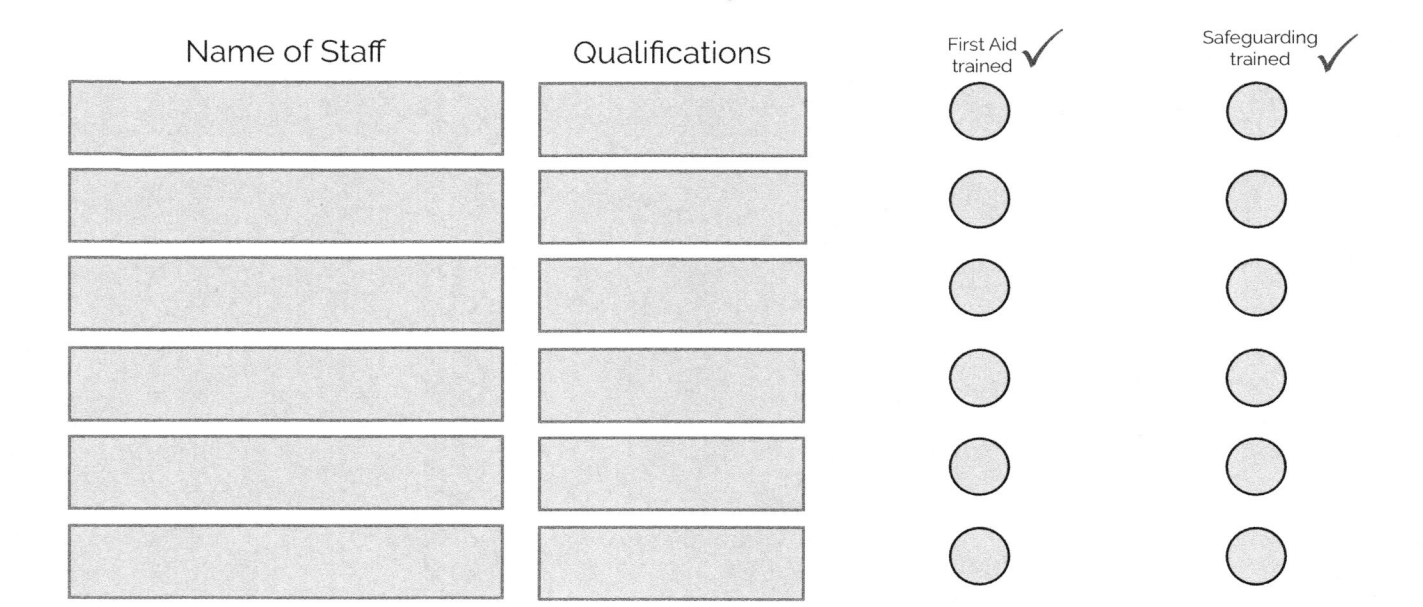

Staffing

Name of Staff	Qualifications	First Aid trained ✓	Safeguarding trained ✓
		◯	◯
		◯	◯
		◯	◯
		◯	◯
		◯	◯
		◯	◯

Jigsaw EARLY YEARS CONSULTANCY

Date

Name of room	Age of room	Ratio in room
		:

Number of children in today	Number of children with EAL	Number of children with SEN	Number of 2 year old funded children	Number of 3 year old funded children

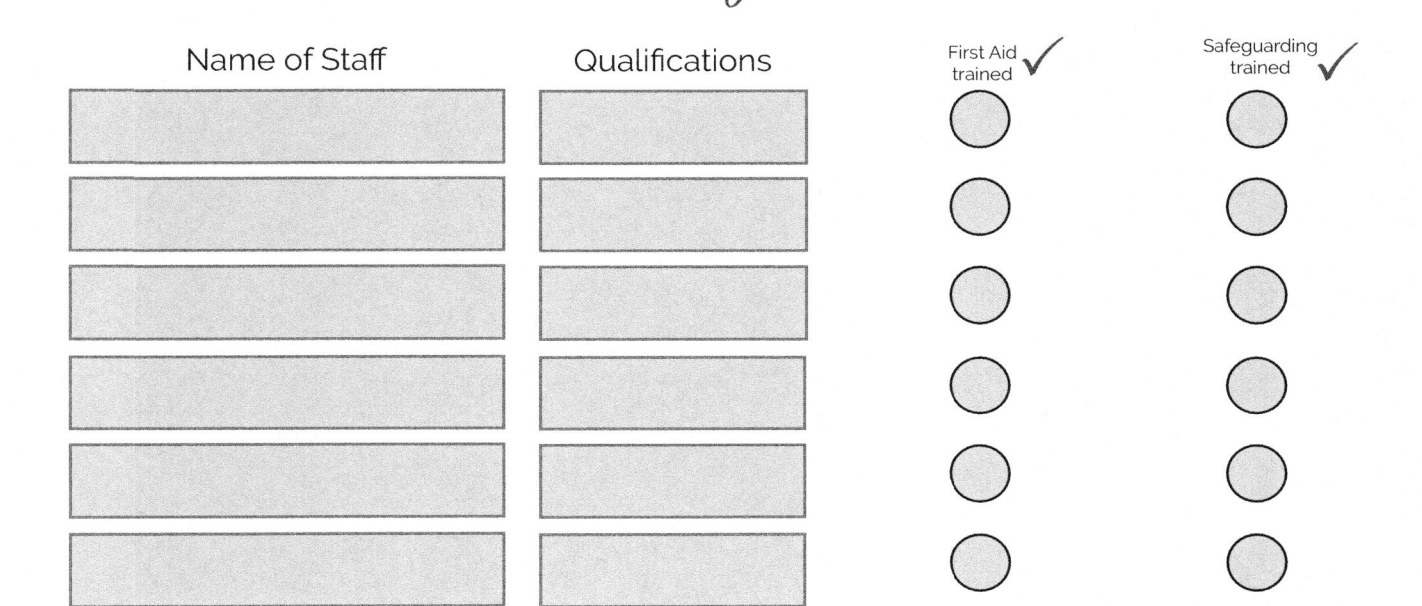

Staffing

Name of Staff	Qualifications	First Aid trained ✓	Safeguarding trained ✓
		○	○
		○	○
		○	○
		○	○
		○	○
		○	○

Date

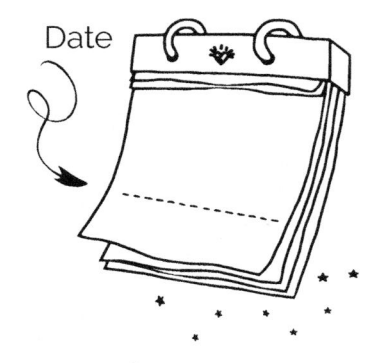

Name of room	Age of room	Ratio in room
		:

Number of children in today	Number of children with EAL	Number of children with SEN	Number of 2 year old funded children	Number of 3 year old funded children

Staffing

Name of Staff	Qualifications	First Aid trained ✓	Safeguarding trained ✓
		○	○
		○	○
		○	○
		○	○
		○	○
		○	○

Date

Jigsaw
EARLY YEARS CONSULTANCY

Name of room	Age of room	Ratio in room
		:

Number of children in today	Number of children with EAL	Number of children with SEN	Number of 2 year old funded children	Number of 3 year old funded children

Staffing

Name of Staff	Qualifications	First Aid trained ✓	Safeguarding trained ✓
		◯	◯
		◯	◯
		◯	◯
		◯	◯
		◯	◯
		◯	◯

Jigsaw
EARLY YEARS CONSULTANCY

Date

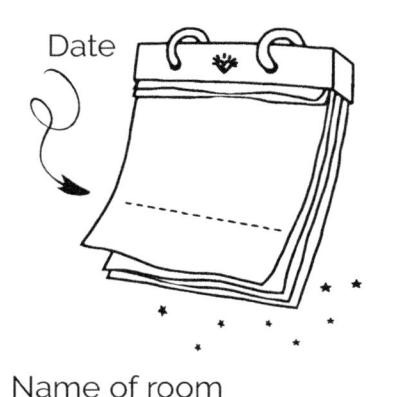

Name of room	Age of room	Ratio in room
		:

Number of children in today	Number of children with EAL	Number of children with SEN	Number of 2 year old funded children	Number of 3 year old funded children

Staffing

Name of Staff	Qualifications	First Aid trained ✓	Safeguarding trained ✓
		○	○
		○	○
		○	○
		○	○
		○	○
		○	○

Date

Name of room

Age of room

Ratio in room

:

Number of children in today	Number of children with EAL	Number of children with SEN	Number of 2 year old funded children	Number of 3 year old funded children

Staffing

Name of Staff	Qualifications	First Aid trained ✓	Safeguarding trained ✓
		○	○
		○	○
		○	○
		○	○
		○	○
		○	○

Jigsaw
EARLY YEARS CONSULTANCY

Date

Name of room	Age of room	Ratio in room
		:

Number of children in today	Number of children with EAL	Number of children with SEN	Number of 2 year old funded children	Number of 3 year old funded children

Staffing

Name of Staff	Qualifications	First Aid trained ✓	Safeguarding trained ✓
		○	○
		○	○
		○	○
		○	○
		○	○
		○	○

Jigsaw
EARLY YEARS CONSULTANCY

Date

Name of room	Age of room	Ratio in room
		:

Number of children in today	Number of children with EAL	Number of children with SEN	Number of 2 year old funded children	Number of 3 year old funded children

Staffing

Name of Staff	Qualifications	First Aid trained ✓	Safeguarding trained ✓
		◯	◯
		◯	◯
		◯	◯
		◯	◯
		◯	◯
		◯	◯

Date

Name of room

Age of room

Ratio in room

Number of children in today	Number of children with EAL	Number of children with SEN	Number of 2 year old funded children	Number of 3 year old funded children

Staffing

Name of Staff	Qualifications	First Aid trained ✓	Safeguarding trained ✓
		○	○
		○	○
		○	○
		○	○
		○	○
		○	○

Date

Name of room	Age of room	Ratio in room
		:

Number of children in today	Number of children with EAL	Number of children with SEN	Number of 2 year old funded children	Number of 3 year old funded children

Staffing

Name of Staff	Qualifications	First Aid trained ✓	Safeguarding trained ✓

Date

Name of room

Age of room

Ratio in room

:

Number of children in today

Number of children with EAL

Number of children with SEN

Number of 2 year old funded children

Number of 3 year old funded children

Staffing

Name of Staff	Qualifications	First Aid trained ✓	Safeguarding trained ✓
		○	○
		○	○
		○	○
		○	○
		○	○
		○	○

Date

Jigsaw
EARLY YEARS CONSULTANCY

Name of room	Age of room	Ratio in room
		:

Number of children in today	Number of children with EAL	Number of children with SEN	Number of 2 year old funded children	Number of 3 year old funded children

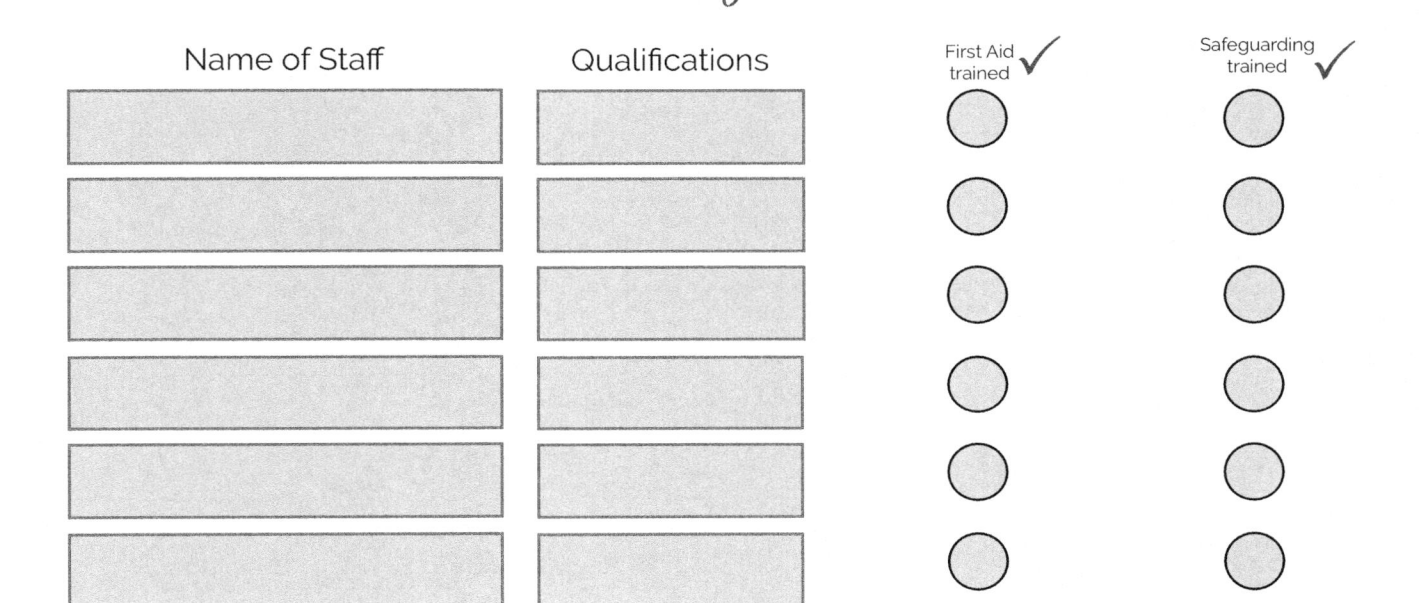

Staffing

Name of Staff	Qualifications	First Aid trained ✓	Safeguarding trained ✓
		○	○
		○	○
		○	○
		○	○
		○	○
		○	○

Date

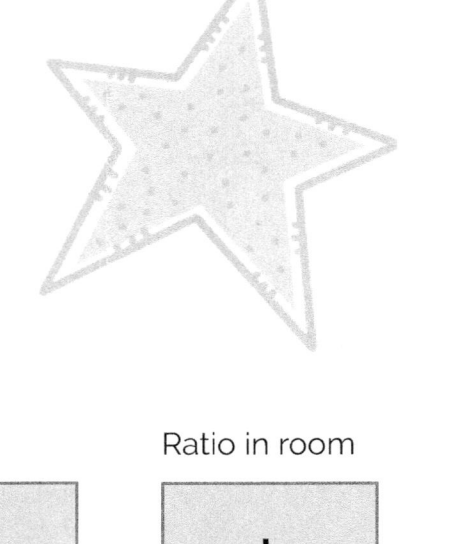

Name of room	Age of room	Ratio in room
		:

Number of children in today	Number of children with EAL	Number of children with SEN	Number of 2 year old funded children	Number of 3 year old funded children

Staffing

Name of Staff	Qualifications	First Aid trained ✓	Safeguarding trained ✓
		○	○
		○	○
		○	○
		○	○
		○	○
		○	○

Date

Name of room

Age of room

Ratio in room

:

Number of children in today

Number of children with EAL

Number of children with SEN

Number of 2 year old funded children

Number of 3 year old funded children

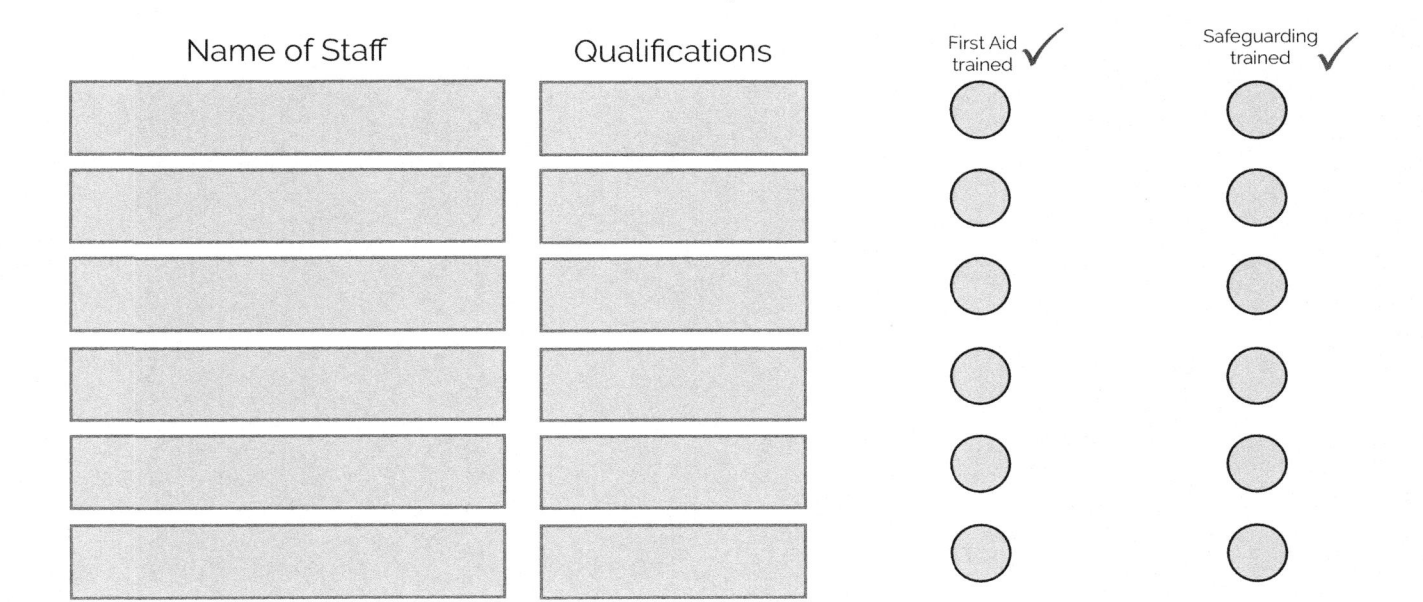

Staffing

Name of Staff	Qualifications	First Aid trained ✓	Safeguarding trained ✓
		○	○
		○	○
		○	○
		○	○
		○	○
		○	○

Date

Jigsaw
EARLY YEARS CONSULTANCY

Name of room

Age of room

Ratio in room

:

Number of children in today

Number of children with EAL

Number of children with SEN

Number of 2 year old funded children

Number of 3 year old funded children

Staffing

Name of Staff	Qualifications	First Aid trained ✓	Safeguarding trained ✓
		○	○
		○	○
		○	○
		○	○
		○	○
		○	○

Jigsaw
EARLY YEARS CONSULTANCY

Date

Name of room	Age of room	Ratio in room
		:

Number of children in today	Number of children with EAL	Number of children with SEN	Number of 2 year old funded children	Number of 3 year old funded children

Staffing

Name of Staff	Qualifications	First Aid trained ✓	Safeguarding trained ✓
		○	○
		○	○
		○	○
		○	○
		○	○
		○	○

Date

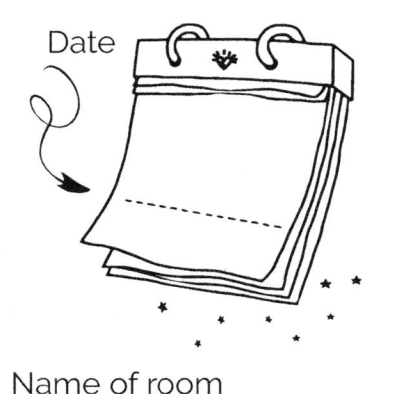

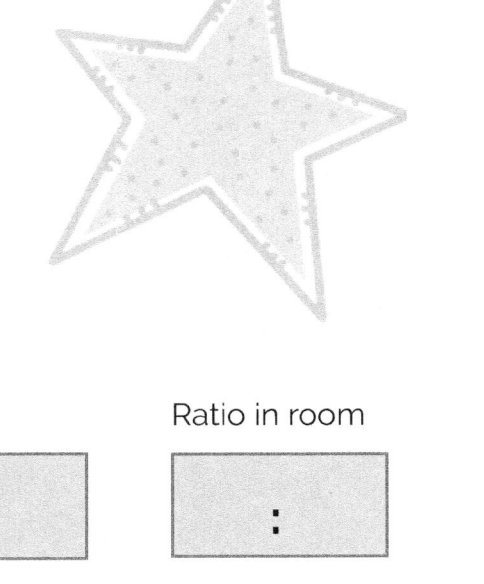

Name of room

Age of room

Ratio in room

Number of children in today	Number of children with EAL	Number of children with SEN	Number of 2 year old funded children	Number of 3 year old funded children

Staffing

Name of Staff	Qualifications	First Aid trained ✓	Safeguarding trained ✓
		○	○
		○	○
		○	○
		○	○
		○	○
		○	○

Date

Name of room

Age of room

Ratio in room

:

Number of children in today

Number of children with EAL

Number of children with SEN

Number of 2 year old funded children

Number of 3 year old funded children

Staffing

Name of Staff	Qualifications	First Aid trained ✓	Safeguarding trained ✓

Jigsaw Early Years Consultancy

Date

Name of room	Age of room	Ratio in room
		:

Number of children in today	Number of children with EAL	Number of children with SEN	Number of 2 year old funded children	Number of 3 year old funded children

Staffing

Name of Staff	Qualifications	First Aid trained ✓	Safeguarding trained ✓

Date

Name of room

Age of room

Ratio in room

:

Number of children in today

Number of children with EAL

Number of children with SEN

Number of 2 year old funded children

Number of 3 year old funded children

Staffing

Name of Staff	Qualifications	First Aid trained ✓	Safeguarding trained ✓

Jigsaw
EARLY YEARS CONSULTANCY

Date

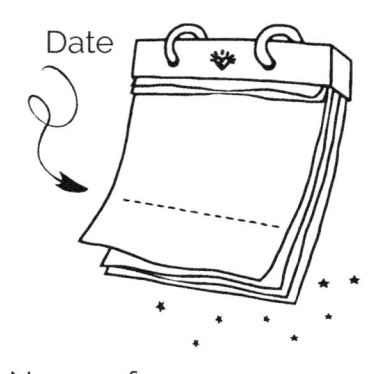

Name of room	Age of room	Ratio in room
		:

Number of children in today	Number of children with EAL	Number of children with SEN	Number of 2 year old funded children	Number of 3 year old funded children

Staffing

Name of Staff	Qualifications	First Aid trained ✓	Safeguarding trained ✓
		◯	◯
		◯	◯
		◯	◯
		◯	◯
		◯	◯
		◯	◯

Date

Name of room

Age of room

Ratio in room

:

Number of children in today

Number of children with EAL

Number of children with SEN

Number of 2 year old funded children

Number of 3 year old funded children

Staffing

Name of Staff	Qualifications	First Aid trained ✓	Safeguarding trained ✓
		○	○
		○	○
		○	○
		○	○
		○	○
		○	○

Jigsaw Early Years Consultancy

Date

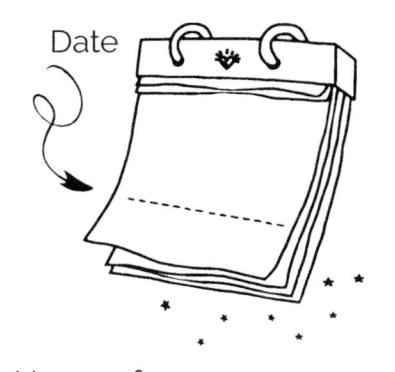

Name of room	Age of room	Ratio in room
		:

Number of children in today	Number of children with EAL	Number of children with SEN	Number of 2 year old funded children	Number of 3 year old funded children

Staffing

Name of Staff	Qualifications	First Aid trained ✓	Safeguarding trained ✓
		○	○
		○	○
		○	○
		○	○
		○	○
		○	○

Date

Name of room	Age of room	Ratio in room
		:

Number of children in today	Number of children with EAL	Number of children with SEN	Number of 2 year old funded children	Number of 3 year old funded children

Staffing

Name of Staff	Qualifications	First Aid trained ✓	Safeguarding trained ✓
		○	○
		○	○
		○	○
		○	○
		○	○
		○	○

Date

Name of room	Age of room	Ratio in room
		:

Number of children in today	Number of children with EAL	Number of children with SEN	Number of 2 year old funded children	Number of 3 year old funded children

Staffing

Name of Staff	Qualifications	First Aid trained ✓	Safeguarding trained ✓
		○	○
		○	○
		○	○
		○	○
		○	○
		○	○

Date

Name of room

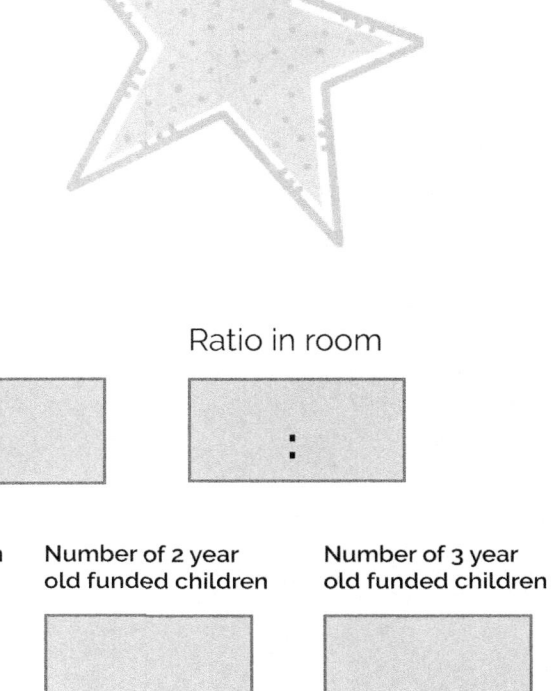

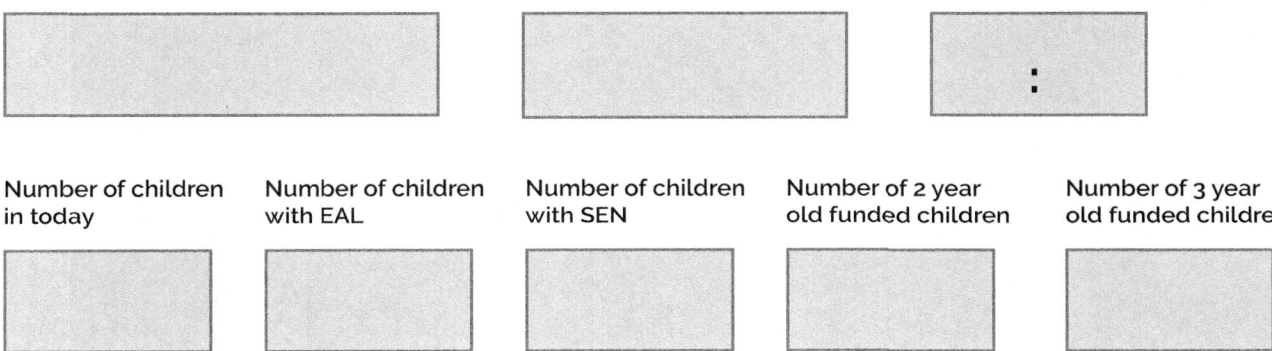

Age of room

Ratio in room

:

Number of children in today

Number of children with EAL

Number of children with SEN

Number of 2 year old funded children

Number of 3 year old funded children

Staffing

Name of Staff	Qualifications	First Aid trained ✓	Safeguarding trained ✓

Jigsaw
EARLY YEARS CONSULTANCY

Date

Name of room	Age of room	Ratio in room
		:

Number of children in today	Number of children with EAL	Number of children with SEN	Number of 2 year old funded children	Number of 3 year old funded children

Staffing

Name of Staff	Qualifications	First Aid trained ✓	Safeguarding trained ✓
		◯	◯
		◯	◯
		◯	◯
		◯	◯
		◯	◯
		◯	◯

Date

Name of room

Age of room

Ratio in room

:

Number of children in today

Number of children with EAL

Number of children with SEN

Number of 2 year old funded children

Number of 3 year old funded children

Staffing

Name of Staff	Qualifications	First Aid trained ✓	Safeguarding trained ✓

Date

Jigsaw
EARLY YEARS CONSULTANCY

Name of room

Age of room

Ratio in room

:

Number of children in today

Number of children with EAL

Number of children with SEN

Number of 2 year old funded children

Number of 3 year old funded children

Staffing

Name of Staff	Qualifications	First Aid trained ✓	Safeguarding trained ✓

Date

Name of room	Age of room	Ratio in room
		:

Number of children in today	Number of children with EAL	Number of children with SEN	Number of 2 year old funded children	Number of 3 year old funded children

Staffing

Name of Staff	Qualifications	First Aid trained ✓	Safeguarding trained ✓
		○	○
		○	○
		○	○
		○	○
		○	○
		○	○

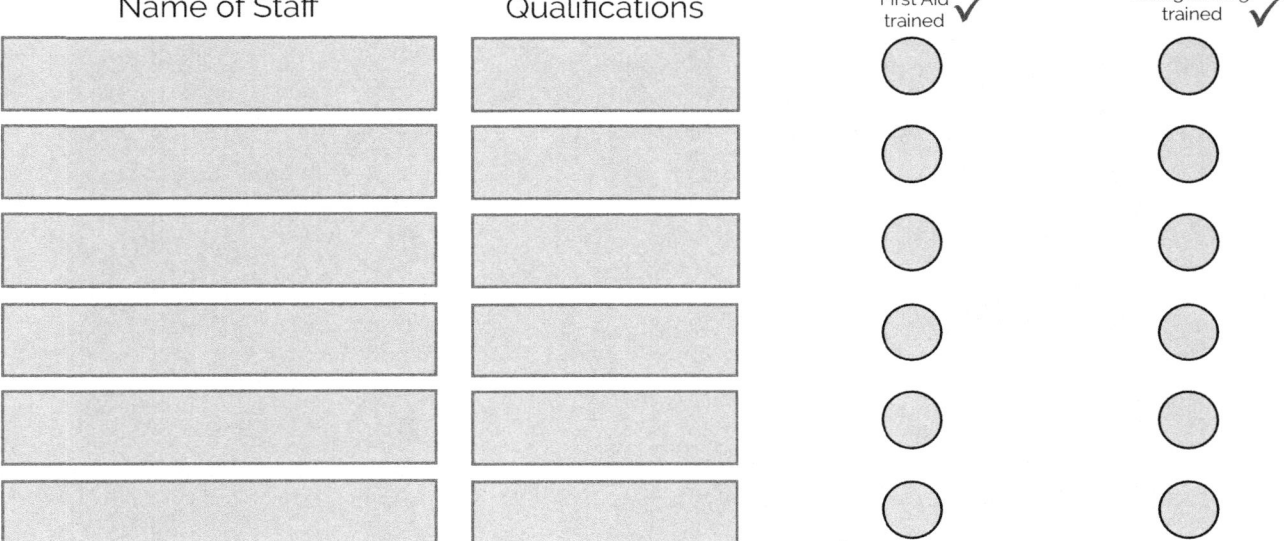

Date

Name of room

Age of room

Ratio in room

Number of children in today	Number of children with EAL	Number of children with SEN	Number of 2 year old funded children	Number of 3 year old funded children

Staffing

Name of Staff	Qualifications	First Aid trained ✓	Safeguarding trained ✓
		○	○
		○	○
		○	○
		○	○
		○	○
		○	○

Jigsaw
EARLY YEARS CONSULTANCY

Date

Name of room	Age of room	Ratio in room
		:

Number of children in today	Number of children with EAL	Number of children with SEN	Number of 2 year old funded children	Number of 3 year old funded children

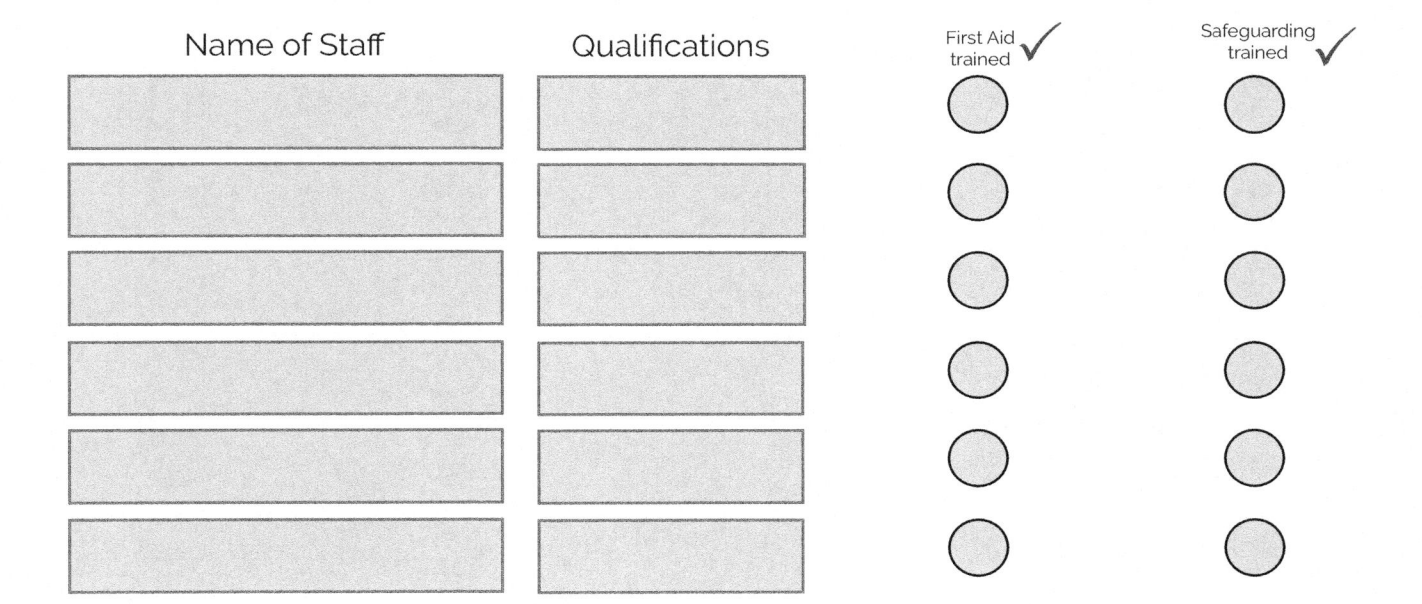

Staffing

Name of Staff	Qualifications	First Aid trained ✓	Safeguarding trained ✓
		○	○
		○	○
		○	○
		○	○
		○	○
		○	○

Date

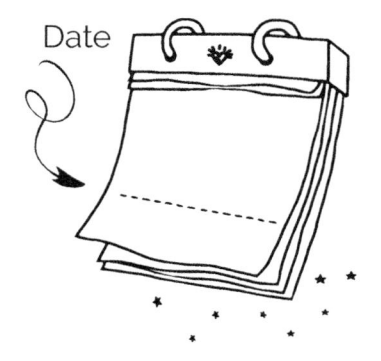

Name of room

Age of room

Ratio in room

:

Number of children in today

Number of children with EAL

Number of children with SEN

Number of 2 year old funded children

Number of 3 year old funded children

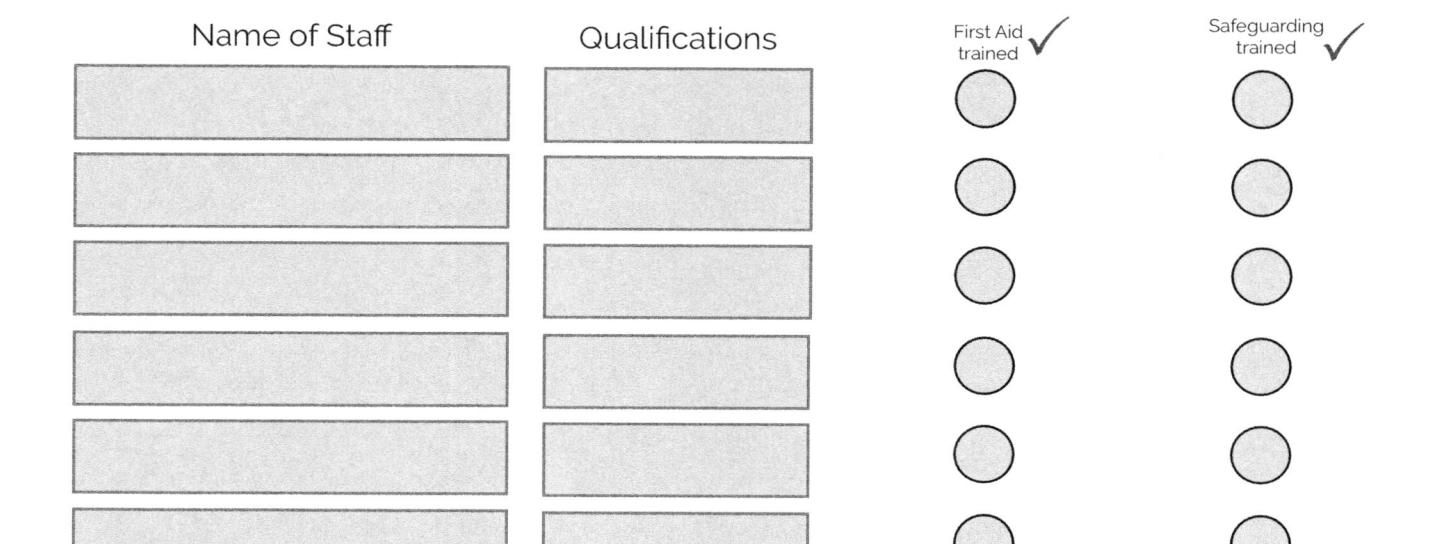

Staffing

Name of Staff	Qualifications	First Aid trained ✓	Safeguarding trained ✓
		○	○
		○	○
		○	○
		○	○
		○	○
		○	○

Jigsaw
EARLY YEARS CONSULTANCY

Date

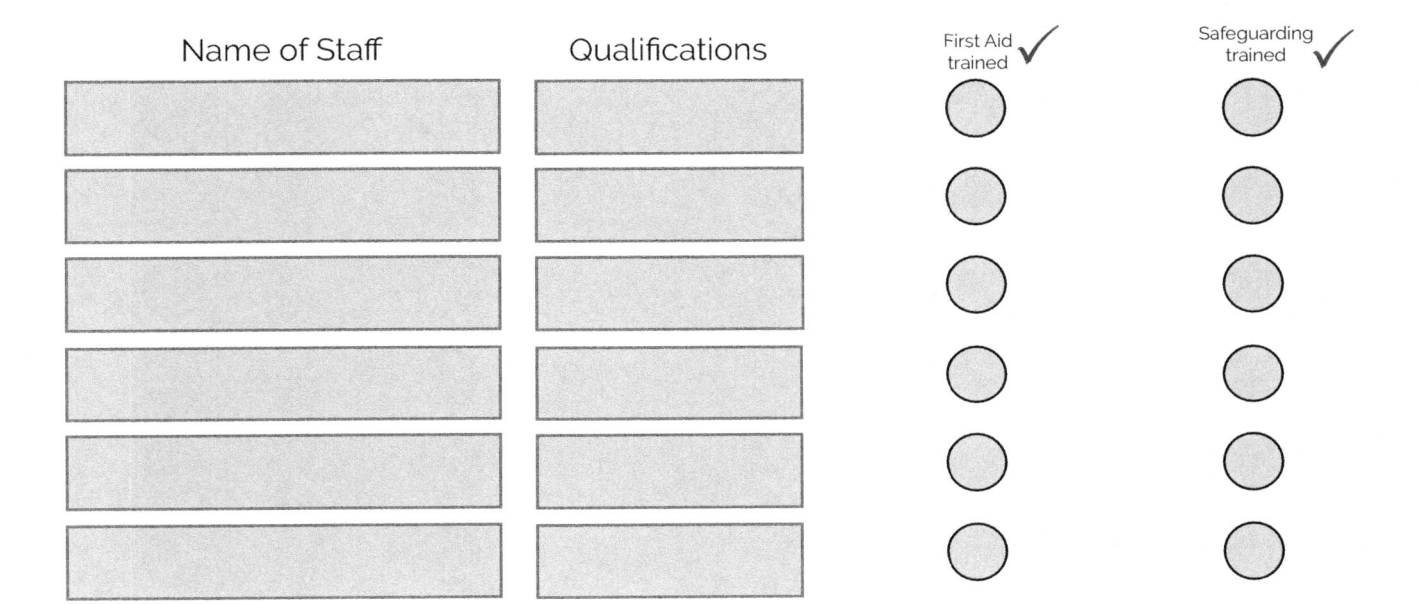

Name of room	Age of room	Ratio in room
		:

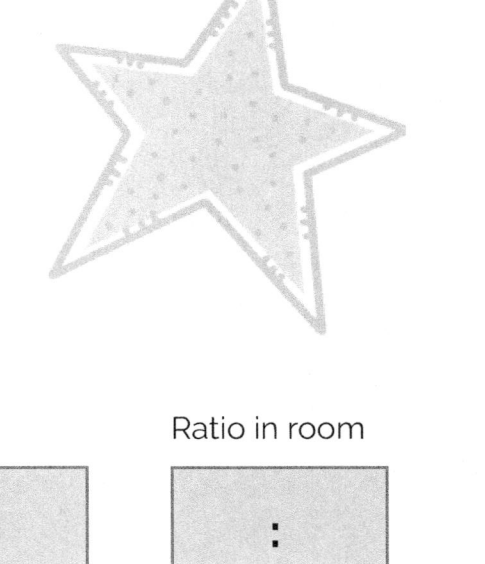

Number of children in today	Number of children with EAL	Number of children with SEN	Number of 2 year old funded children	Number of 3 year old funded children

Staffing

Name of Staff	Qualifications	First Aid trained ✓	Safeguarding trained ✓
		○	○
		○	○
		○	○
		○	○
		○	○
		○	○

Jigsaw
EARLY YEARS CONSULTANCY

Date

Name of room	Age of room	Ratio in room
		:

Number of children in today	Number of children with EAL	Number of children with SEN	Number of 2 year old funded children	Number of 3 year old funded children

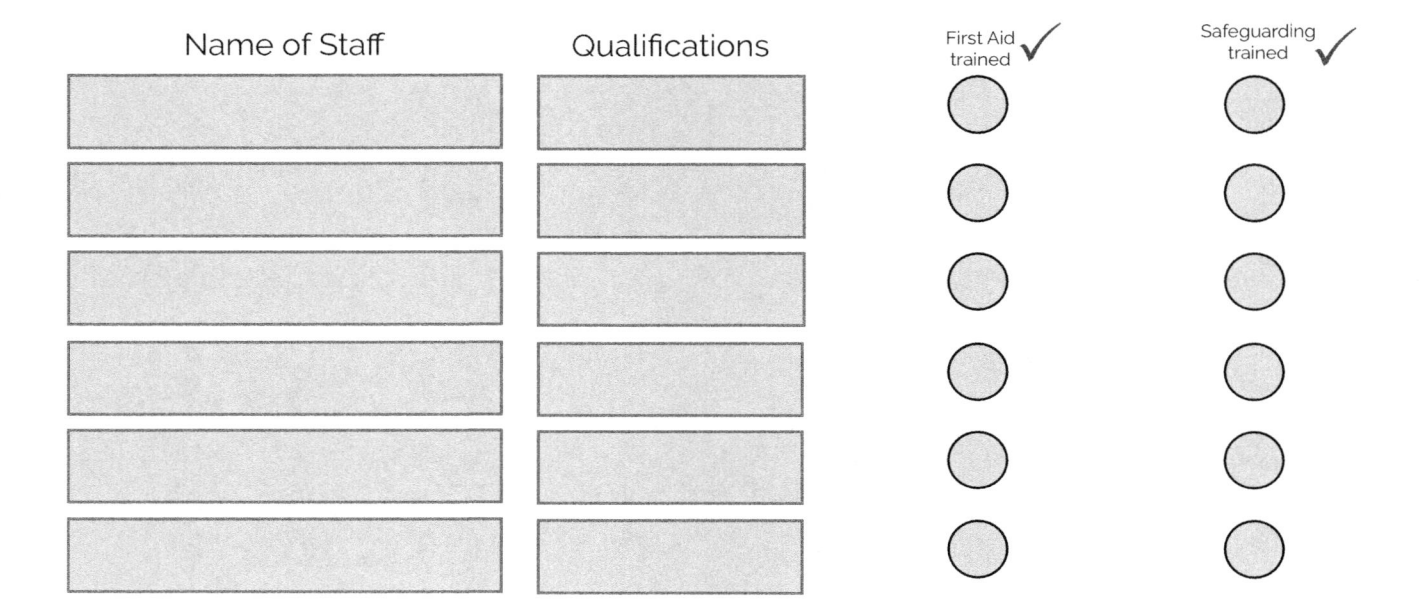

Staffing

Name of Staff	Qualifications	First Aid trained ✓	Safeguarding trained ✓
		○	○
		○	○
		○	○
		○	○
		○	○
		○	○

Date

Name of room	Age of room	Ratio in room
		:

Number of children in today	Number of children with EAL	Number of children with SEN	Number of 2 year old funded children	Number of 3 year old funded children

Staffing

Name of Staff	Qualifications	First Aid trained ✓	Safeguarding trained ✓
		◯	◯
		◯	◯
		◯	◯
		◯	◯
		◯	◯
		◯	◯

Date

Jigsaw
EARLY YEARS CONSULTANCY

Name of room

Age of room

Ratio in room

Number of children in today	Number of children with EAL	Number of children with SEN	Number of 2 year old funded children	Number of 3 year old funded children

Staffing

Name of Staff	Qualifications	First Aid trained ✓	Safeguarding trained ✓
		○	○
		○	○
		○	○
		○	○
		○	○
		○	○

Date

Name of room

Age of room

Ratio in room

Number of children in today	Number of children with EAL	Number of children with SEN	Number of 2 year old funded children	Number of 3 year old funded children

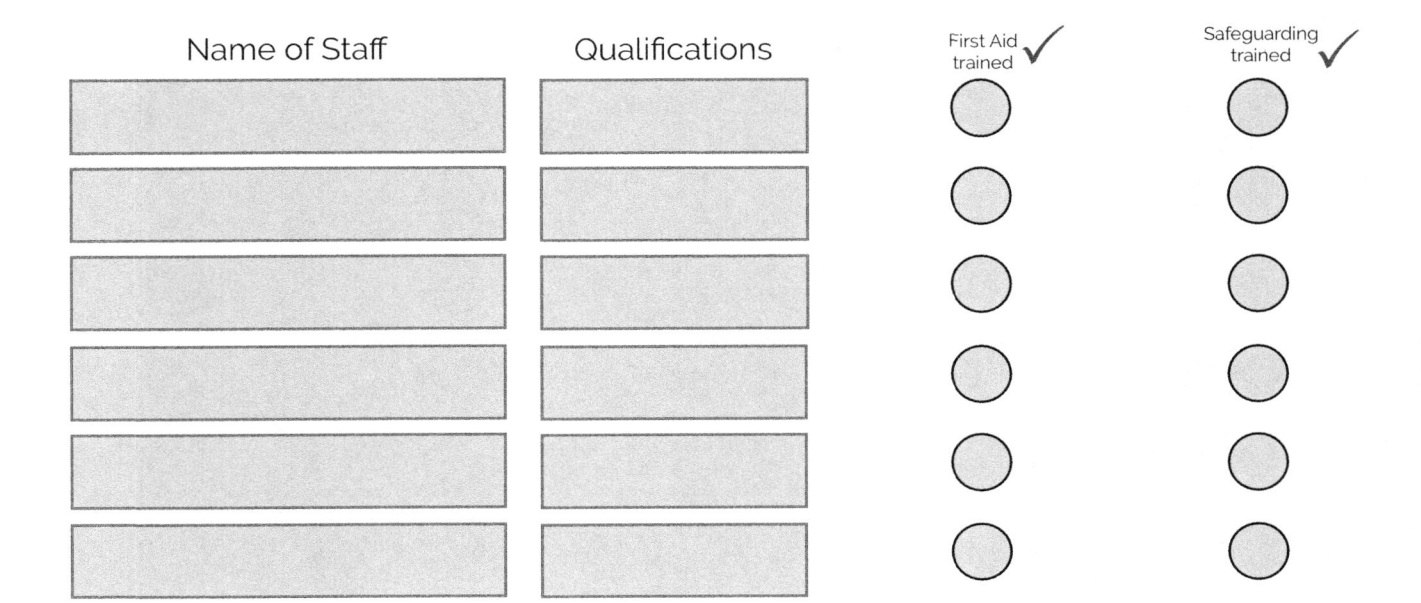

Staffing

Name of Staff	Qualifications	First Aid trained ✓	Safeguarding trained ✓

Date

Name of room

Age of room

Ratio in room

:

Number of children in today

Number of children with EAL

Number of children with SEN

Number of 2 year old funded children

Number of 3 year old funded children

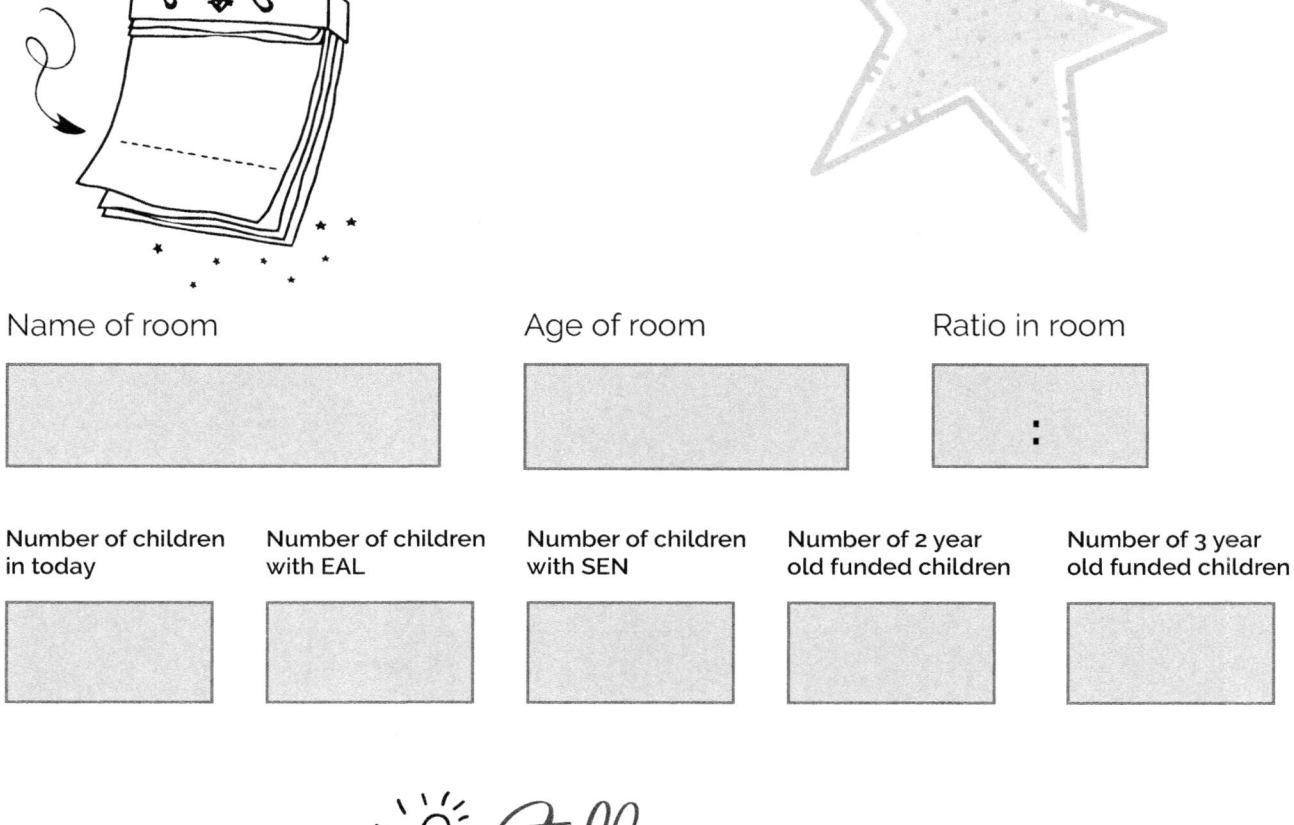

Staffing

Name of Staff	Qualifications	First Aid trained ✓	Safeguarding trained ✓
		◯	◯
		◯	◯
		◯	◯
		◯	◯
		◯	◯
		◯	◯

Date

Name of room

Age of room

Ratio in room

:

Number of children in today

Number of children with EAL

Number of children with SEN

Number of 2 year old funded children

Number of 3 year old funded children

Staffing

Name of Staff	Qualifications	First Aid trained ✓	Safeguarding trained ✓
		○	○
		○	○
		○	○
		○	○
		○	○
		○	○

Jigsaw
EARLY YEARS CONSULTANCY

Date

Name of room	Age of room	Ratio in room
		:

Number of children in today	Number of children with EAL	Number of children with SEN	Number of 2 year old funded children	Number of 3 year old funded children

Staffing

Name of Staff	Qualifications	First Aid trained ✓	Safeguarding trained ✓
		○	○
		○	○
		○	○
		○	○
		○	○
		○	○

Date

Jigsaw
EARLY YEARS CONSULTANCY

Name of room	Age of room	Ratio in room
		:

Number of children in today	Number of children with EAL	Number of children with SEN	Number of 2 year old funded children	Number of 3 year old funded children

Staffing

Name of Staff	Qualifications	First Aid trained ✓	Safeguarding trained ✓
		○	○
		○	○
		○	○
		○	○
		○	○
		○	○

Date

Name of room

Age of room

Ratio in room

Number of children in today	Number of children with EAL	Number of children with SEN	Number of 2 year old funded children	Number of 3 year old funded children

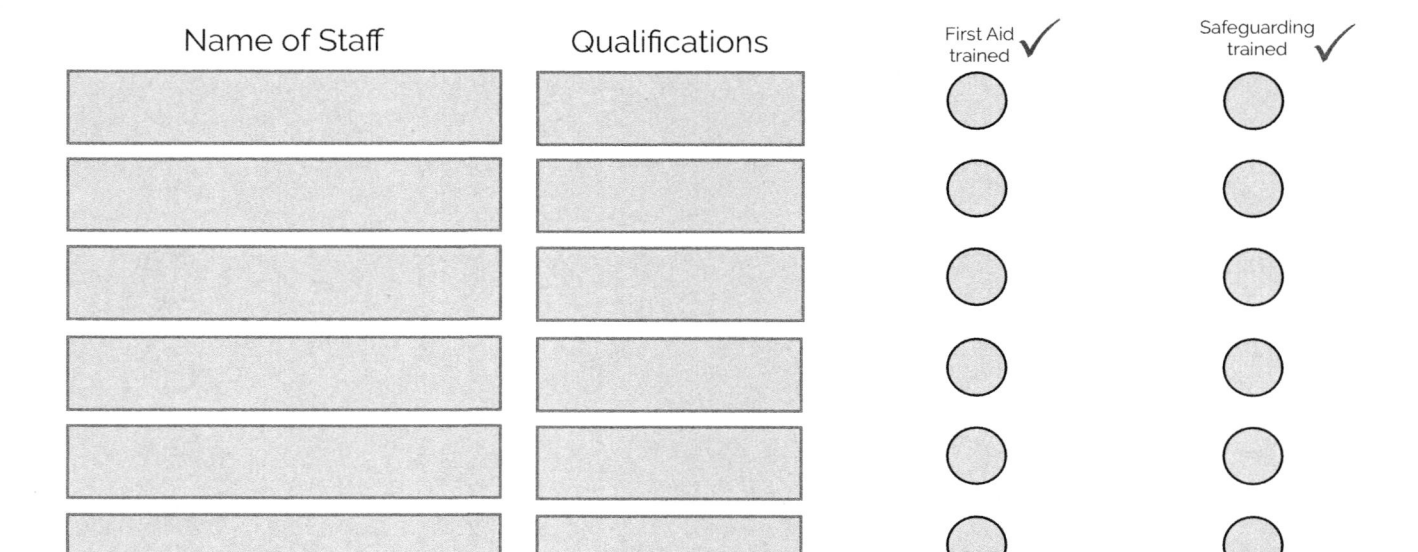

Staffing

Name of Staff	Qualifications	First Aid trained ✓	Safeguarding trained ✓

Jigsaw
EARLY YEARS CONSULTANCY

Date

Name of room	Age of room	Ratio in room
		:

Number of children in today	Number of children with EAL	Number of children with SEN	Number of 2 year old funded children	Number of 3 year old funded children

Staffing

Name of Staff	Qualifications	First Aid trained ✓	Safeguarding trained ✓

Date

Jigsaw
EARLY YEARS CONSULTANCY

Name of room	Age of room	Ratio in room
		:

Number of children in today	Number of children with EAL	Number of children with SEN	Number of 2 year old funded children	Number of 3 year old funded children

Staffing

Name of Staff	Qualifications	First Aid trained ✓	Safeguarding trained ✓
		○	○
		○	○
		○	○
		○	○
		○	○
		○	○

Date

Name of room

Age of room

Ratio in room

:

Number of children in today

Number of children with EAL

Number of children with SEN

Number of 2 year old funded children

Number of 3 year old funded children

Staffing

Name of Staff	Qualifications	First Aid trained ✓	Safeguarding trained ✓
		○	○
		○	○
		○	○
		○	○
		○	○
		○	○

Date

Name of room

Age of room

Ratio in room

:

Number of children in today	Number of children with EAL	Number of children with SEN	Number of 2 year old funded children	Number of 3 year old funded children

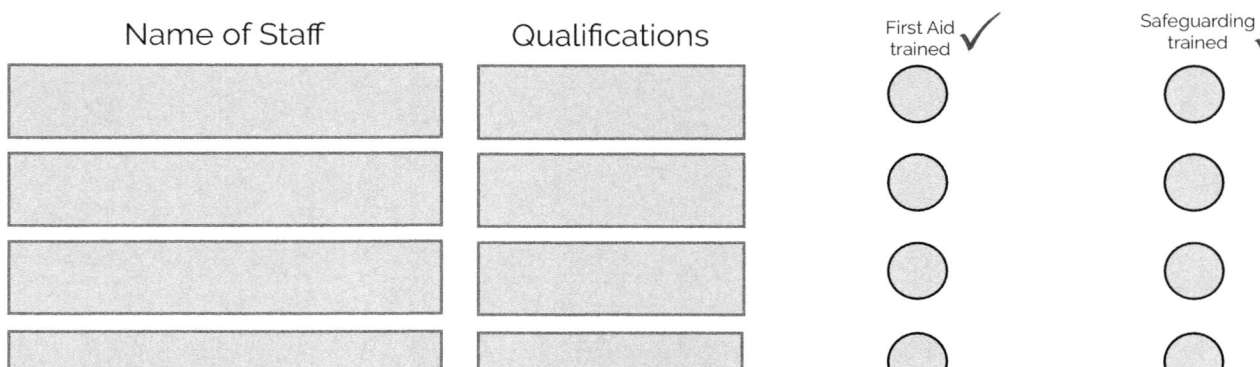

Staffing

Name of Staff	Qualifications	First Aid trained ✓	Safeguarding trained ✓

Date

Name of room

Age of room

Ratio in room

:

Number of children in today	Number of children with EAL	Number of children with SEN	Number of 2 year old funded children	Number of 3 year old funded children

Staffing

Name of Staff	Qualifications	First Aid trained ✓	Safeguarding trained ✓

Jigsaw
EARLY YEARS CONSULTANCY

Date

Name of room

Age of room

Ratio in room

Number of children in today	Number of children with EAL	Number of children with SEN	Number of 2 year old funded children	Number of 3 year old funded children

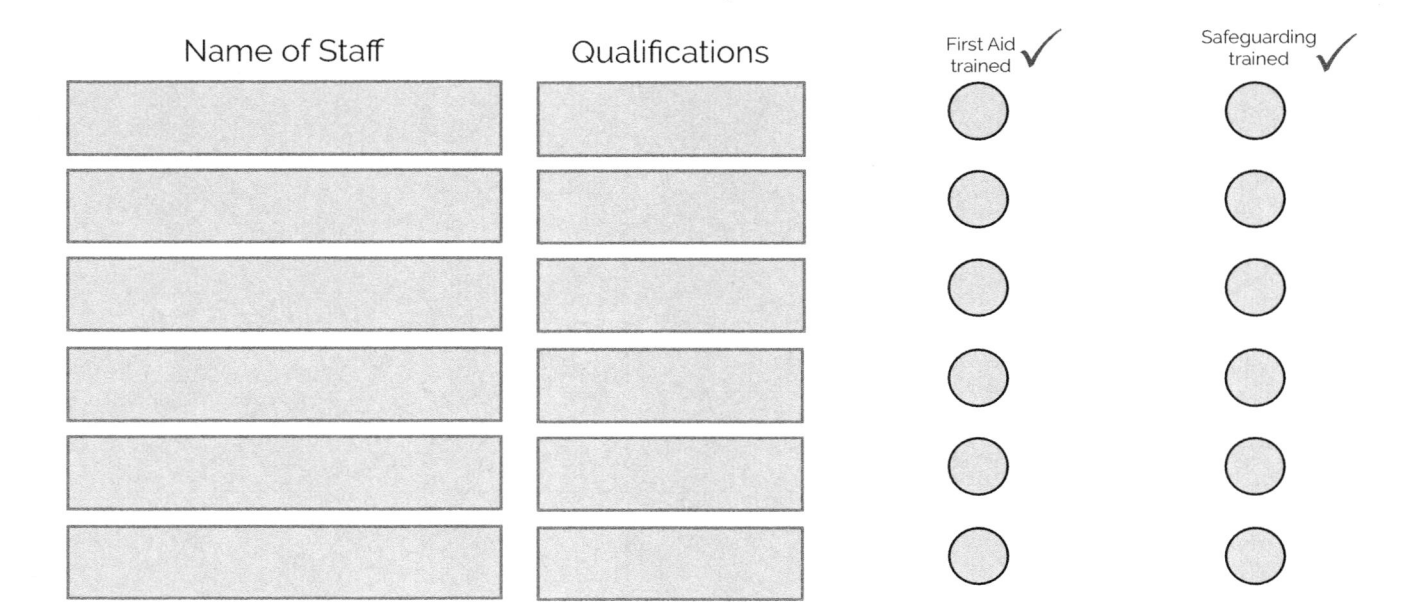

Staffing

Name of Staff	Qualifications	First Aid trained ✓	Safeguarding trained ✓
		○	○
		○	○
		○	○
		○	○
		○	○
		○	○

Date

Name of room

Age of room

Ratio in room

:

Number of children in today	Number of children with EAL	Number of children with SEN	Number of 2 year old funded children	Number of 3 year old funded children

Staffing

Name of Staff	Qualifications	First Aid trained ✓	Safeguarding trained ✓

Jigsaw Early Years Consultancy

Date

Name of room

Age of room

Ratio in room

:

Number of children in today	Number of children with EAL	Number of children with SEN	Number of 2 year old funded children	Number of 3 year old funded children

Staffing

Name of Staff	Qualifications	First Aid trained ✓	Safeguarding trained ✓

Date

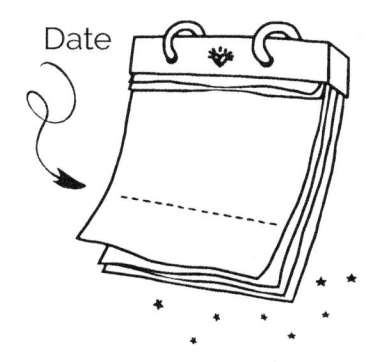

Name of room

Age of room

Ratio in room

:

Number of children in today

Number of children with EAL

Number of children with SEN

Number of 2 year old funded children

Number of 3 year old funded children

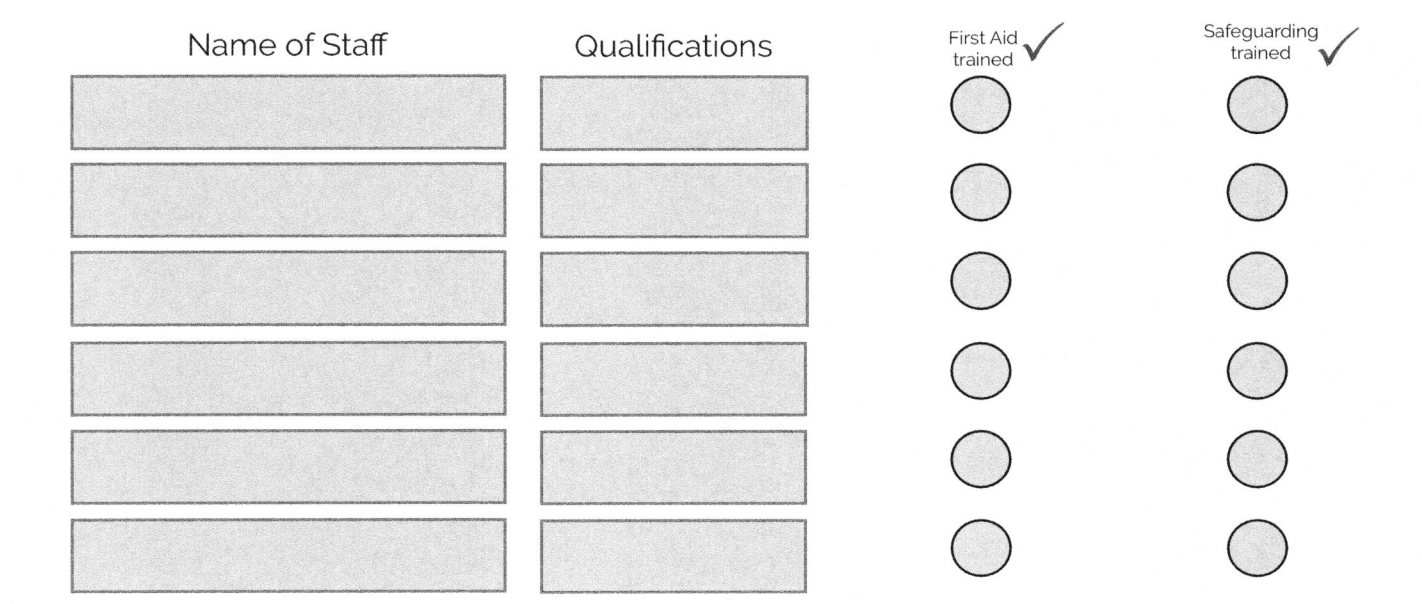

Staffing

Name of Staff	Qualifications	First Aid trained ✓	Safeguarding trained ✓

Date

Name of room

Age of room

Ratio in room

Number of children in today	Number of children with EAL	Number of children with SEN	Number of 2 year old funded children	Number of 3 year old funded children

Staffing

Name of Staff	Qualifications	First Aid trained ✓	Safeguarding trained ✓

Date

Name of room

Age of room

Ratio in room

Number of children in today	Number of children with EAL	Number of children with SEN	Number of 2 year old funded children	Number of 3 year old funded children

Staffing

Name of Staff	Qualifications	First Aid trained ✓	Safeguarding trained ✓

Date

Name of room	Age of room	Ratio in room
		:

Number of children in today	Number of children with EAL	Number of children with SEN	Number of 2 year old funded children	Number of 3 year old funded children

Staffing

Name of Staff	Qualifications	First Aid trained ✓	Safeguarding trained ✓

Date

Name of room

Age of room

Ratio in room

Number of children in today

Number of children with EAL

Number of children with SEN

Number of 2 year old funded children

Number of 3 year old funded children

Staffing

Name of Staff	Qualifications	First Aid trained ✓	Safeguarding trained ✓
		◯	◯
		◯	◯
		◯	◯
		◯	◯
		◯	◯
		◯	◯

Date

Name of room

Age of room

Ratio in room

:

Number of children in today

Number of children with EAL

Number of children with SEN

Number of 2 year old funded children

Number of 3 year old funded children

Staffing

Name of Staff	Qualifications	First Aid trained ✓	Safeguarding trained ✓
		◯	◯
		◯	◯
		◯	◯
		◯	◯
		◯	◯
		◯	◯

Jigsaw
EARLY YEARS CONSULTANCY

Date

Name of room	Age of room	Ratio in room
		:

Number of children in today	Number of children with EAL	Number of children with SEN	Number of 2 year old funded children	Number of 3 year old funded children

Staffing

Name of Staff	Qualifications	First Aid trained ✓	Safeguarding trained ✓
		○	○
		○	○
		○	○
		○	○
		○	○
		○	○

Jigsaw
EARLY YEARS CONSULTANCY

Date

Name of room	Age of room	Ratio in room
		:

Number of children in today	Number of children with EAL	Number of children with SEN	Number of 2 year old funded children	Number of 3 year old funded children

Staffing

Name of Staff	Qualifications	First Aid trained ✓	Safeguarding trained ✓
		○	○
		○	○
		○	○
		○	○
		○	○
		○	○

Jigsaw
EARLY YEARS CONSULTANCY

Date

Name of room

Age of room

Ratio in room

:

Number of children in today

Number of children with EAL

Number of children with SEN

Number of 2 year old funded children

Number of 3 year old funded children

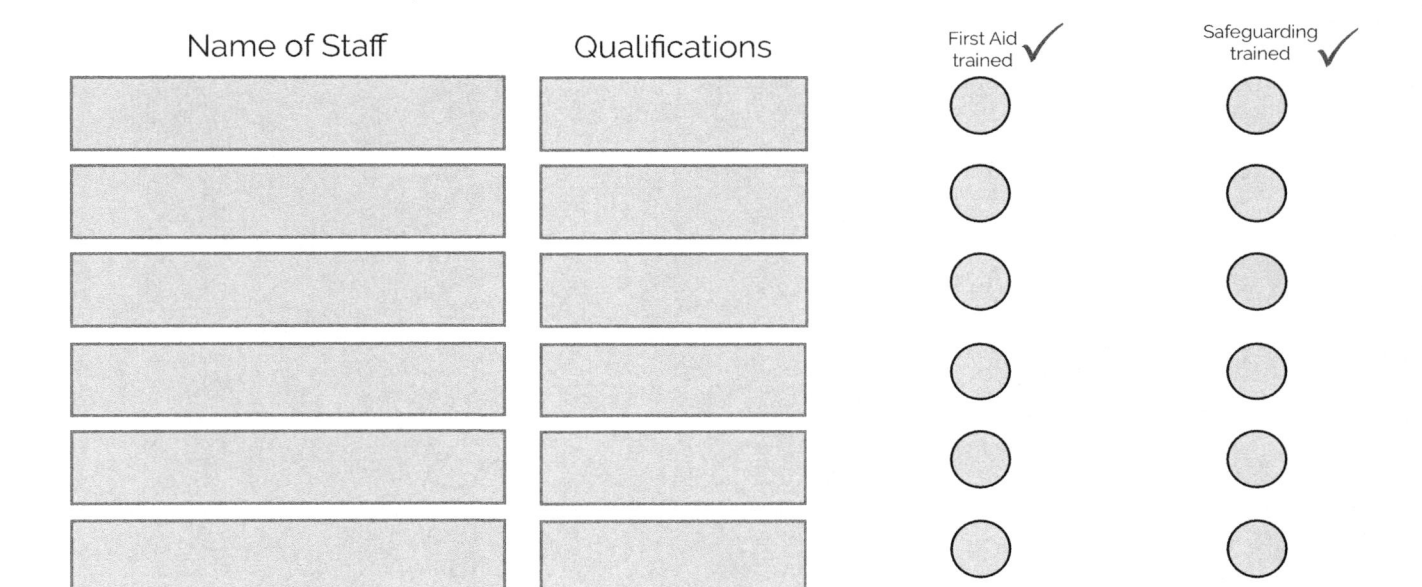

Staffing

Name of Staff	Qualifications	First Aid trained ✓	Safeguarding trained ✓
		○	○
		○	○
		○	○
		○	○
		○	○
		○	○

Jigsaw
EARLY YEARS CONSULTANCY

Date

Name of room	Age of room	Ratio in room
		:

Number of children in today	Number of children with EAL	Number of children with SEN	Number of 2 year old funded children	Number of 3 year old funded children

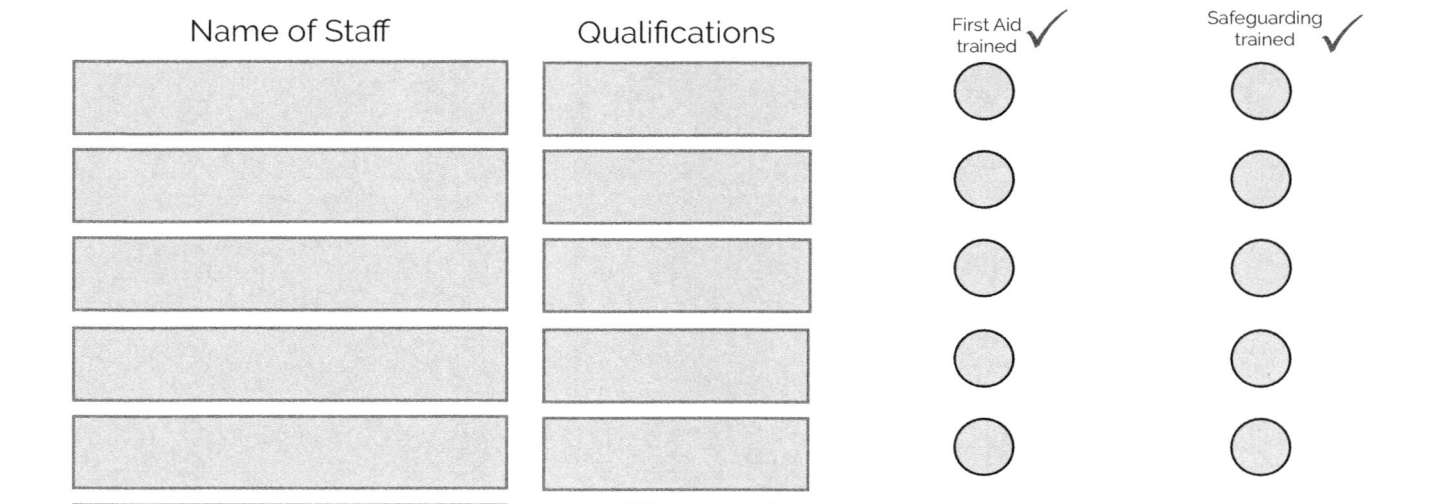

Staffing

Name of Staff	Qualifications	First Aid trained ✓	Safeguarding trained ✓
		○	○
		○	○
		○	○
		○	○
		○	○
		○	○

Jigsaw
EARLY YEARS CONSULTANCY

Date

Name of room	Age of room	Ratio in room
		:

Number of children in today	Number of children with EAL	Number of children with SEN	Number of 2 year old funded children	Number of 3 year old funded children

Staffing

Name of Staff	Qualifications	First Aid trained ✓	Safeguarding trained ✓
		◯	◯
		◯	◯
		◯	◯
		◯	◯
		◯	◯
		◯	◯

Jigsaw
EARLY YEARS CONSULTANCY

Date

Name of room

Age of room

Ratio in room

:

Number of children in today

Number of children with EAL

Number of children with SEN

Number of 2 year old funded children

Number of 3 year old funded children

Staffing

Name of Staff	Qualifications	First Aid trained ✓	Safeguarding trained ✓
		○	○
		○	○
		○	○
		○	○
		○	○
		○	○

Date

Jigsaw
EARLY YEARS CONSULTANCY

Name of room	Age of room	Ratio in room
		:

Number of children in today	Number of children with EAL	Number of children with SEN	Number of 2 year old funded children	Number of 3 year old funded children

Staffing

Name of Staff	Qualifications	First Aid trained ✓	Safeguarding trained ✓
		○	○
		○	○
		○	○
		○	○
		○	○
		○	○

Date

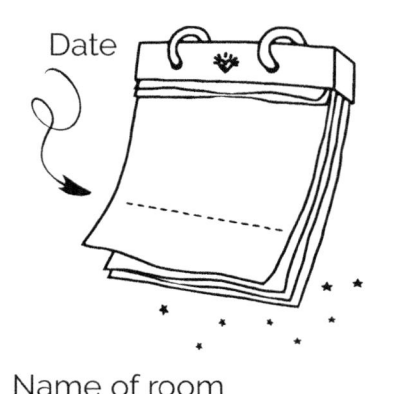

Name of room

Age of room

Ratio in room

Number of children in today

Number of children with EAL

Number of children with SEN

Number of 2 year old funded children

Number of 3 year old funded children

Staffing

Name of Staff	Qualifications	First Aid trained ✓	Safeguarding trained ✓

Date

Name of room	Age of room	Ratio in room
		:

Number of children in today	Number of children with EAL	Number of children with SEN	Number of 2 year old funded children	Number of 3 year old funded children

Staffing

Name of Staff	Qualifications	First Aid trained ✓	Safeguarding trained ✓
		○	○
		○	○
		○	○
		○	○
		○	○
		○	○

Date

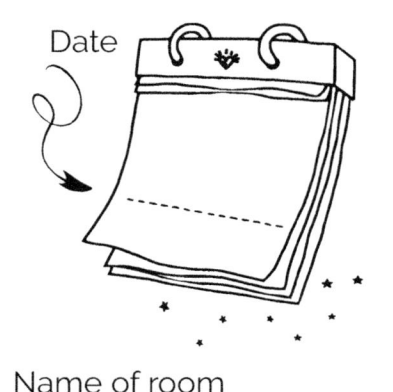

Name of room

Age of room

Ratio in room

:

Number of children in today

Number of children with EAL

Number of children with SEN

Number of 2 year old funded children

Number of 3 year old funded children

Staffing

Name of Staff	Qualifications	First Aid trained ✓	Safeguarding trained ✓
		○	○
		○	○
		○	○
		○	○
		○	○
		○	○

Date

Name of room

Age of room

Ratio in room

:

Number of children in today

Number of children with EAL

Number of children with SEN

Number of 2 year old funded children

Number of 3 year old funded children

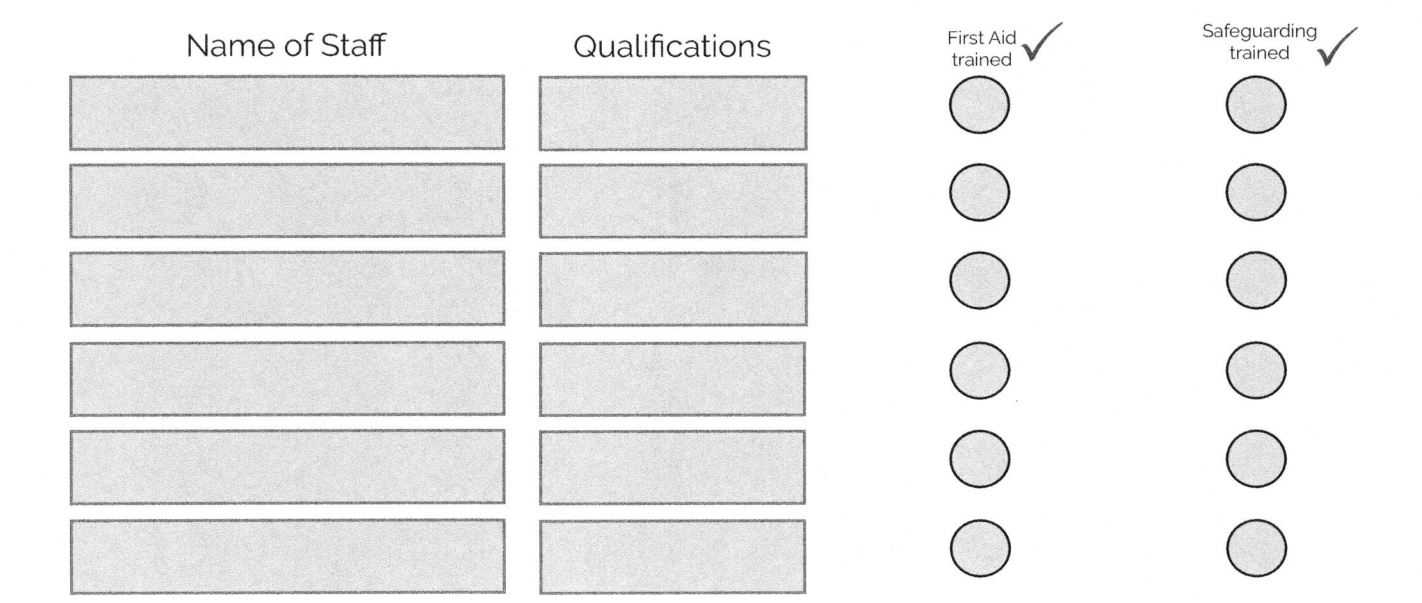

Staffing

Name of Staff	Qualifications	First Aid trained ✓	Safeguarding trained ✓

Date

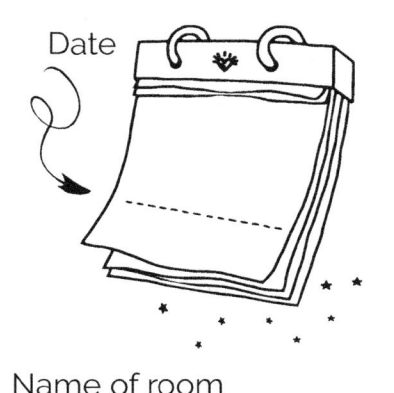

Name of room	Age of room	Ratio in room
		:

Number of children in today	Number of children with EAL	Number of children with SEN	Number of 2 year old funded children	Number of 3 year old funded children

Staffing

Name of Staff	Qualifications	First Aid trained ✓	Safeguarding trained ✓
		◯	◯
		◯	◯
		◯	◯
		◯	◯
		◯	◯
		◯	◯

Date

Name of room

Age of room

Ratio in room

Number of children in today

Number of children with EAL

Number of children with SEN

Number of 2 year old funded children

Number of 3 year old funded children

Staffing

Name of Staff	Qualifications	First Aid trained ✓	Safeguarding trained ✓
		○	○
		○	○
		○	○
		○	○
		○	○
		○	○

Jigsaw Early Years Consultancy

Date

Name of room	Age of room	Ratio in room
		:

Number of children in today	Number of children with EAL	Number of children with SEN	Number of 2 year old funded children	Number of 3 year old funded children

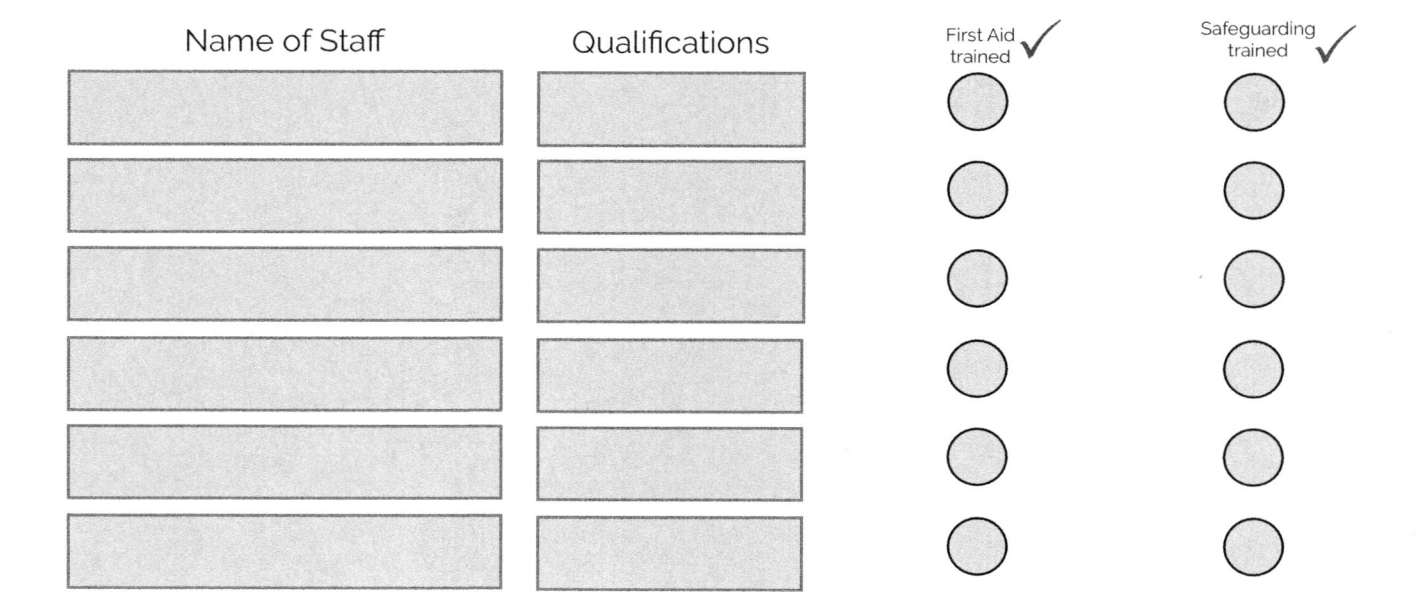

Staffing

Name of Staff	Qualifications	First Aid trained ✓	Safeguarding trained ✓
		○	○
		○	○
		○	○
		○	○
		○	○
		○	○

Jigsaw
EARLY YEARS CONSULTANCY

Date

Name of room	Age of room	Ratio in room
		:

Number of children in today	Number of children with EAL	Number of children with SEN	Number of 2 year old funded children	Number of 3 year old funded children

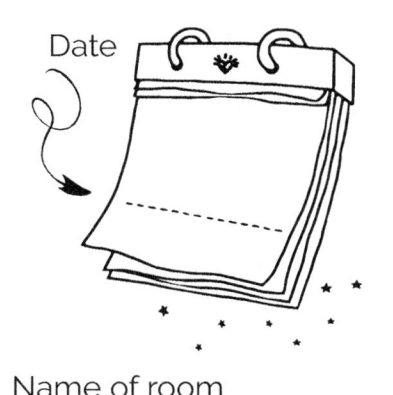

Staffing

Name of Staff	Qualifications	First Aid trained ✓	Safeguarding trained ✓
		○	○
		○	○
		○	○
		○	○
		○	○
		○	○

Date

Name of room

Age of room

Ratio in room

:

Number of children in today	Number of children with EAL	Number of children with SEN	Number of 2 year old funded children	Number of 3 year old funded children

Staffing

Name of Staff	Qualifications	First Aid trained ✓	Safeguarding trained ✓
		○	○
		○	○
		○	○
		○	○
		○	○
		○	○

Jigsaw
EARLY YEARS CONSULTANCY

Date

Name of room

Age of room

Ratio in room

:

Number of children in today

Number of children with EAL

Number of children with SEN

Number of 2 year old funded children

Number of 3 year old funded children

Staffing

Name of Staff	Qualifications	First Aid trained ✓	Safeguarding trained ✓
		◯	◯
		◯	◯
		◯	◯
		◯	◯
		◯	◯
		◯	◯

Jigsaw
EARLY YEARS CONSULTANCY

Date

Name of room	Age of room	Ratio in room
		:

Number of children in today	Number of children with EAL	Number of children with SEN	Number of 2 year old funded children	Number of 3 year old funded children

Staffing

Name of Staff	Qualifications	First Aid trained ✓	Safeguarding trained ✓
		○	○
		○	○
		○	○
		○	○
		○	○
		○	○

Jigsaw
EARLY YEARS CONSULTANCY

Date

Name of room

Age of room

Ratio in room

Number of children in today

Number of children with EAL

Number of children with SEN

Number of 2 year old funded children

Number of 3 year old funded children

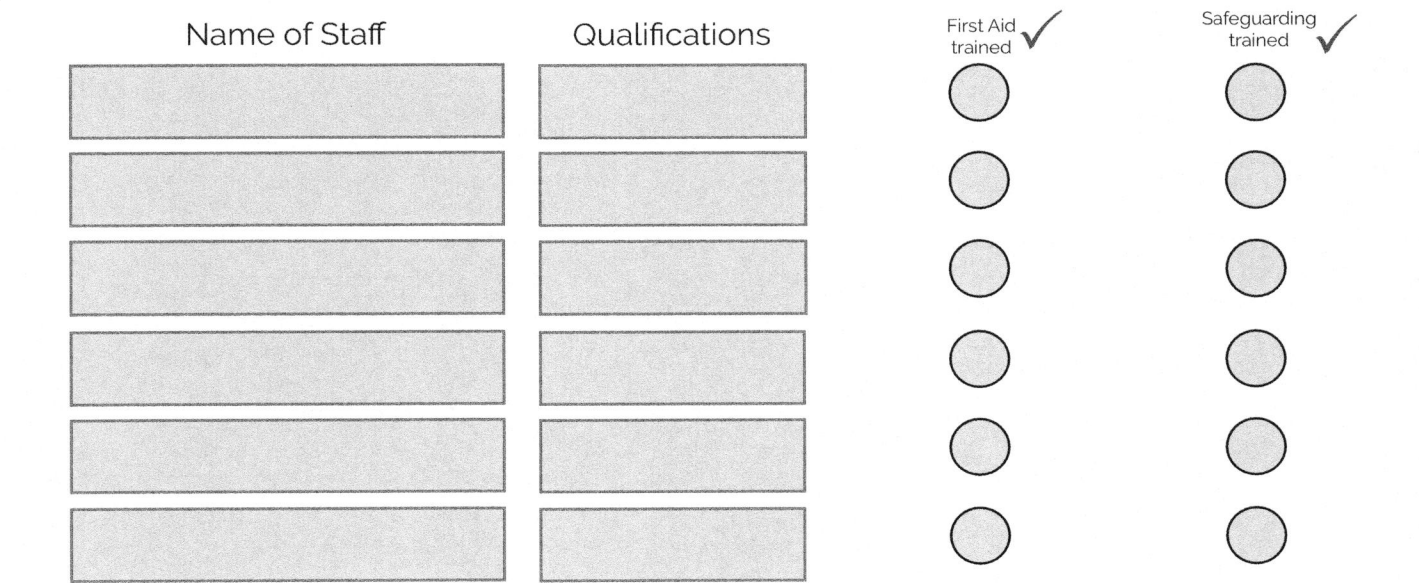

Staffing

Name of Staff	Qualifications	First Aid trained ✓	Safeguarding trained ✓

Date

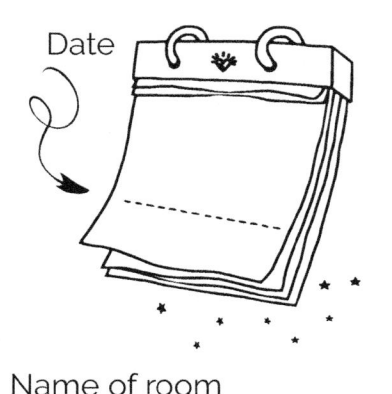

Jigsaw
EARLY YEARS CONSULTANCY

Name of room	Age of room	Ratio in room
		:

Number of children in today	Number of children with EAL	Number of children with SEN	Number of 2 year old funded children	Number of 3 year old funded children

Staffing

Name of Staff	Qualifications	First Aid trained ✓	Safeguarding trained ✓
		○	○
		○	○
		○	○
		○	○
		○	○
		○	○

Jigsaw
EARLY YEARS CONSULTANCY

Date

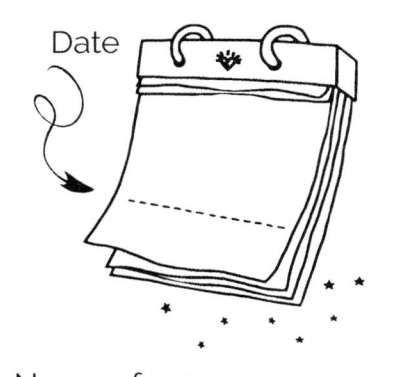

Name of room	Age of room	Ratio in room
		:

Number of children in today	Number of children with EAL	Number of children with SEN	Number of 2 year old funded children	Number of 3 year old funded children

Staffing

Name of Staff	Qualifications	First Aid trained ✓	Safeguarding trained ✓
		◯	◯
		◯	◯
		◯	◯
		◯	◯
		◯	◯
		◯	◯

Date

Name of room

Age of room

Ratio in room

:

Number of children in today

Number of children with EAL

Number of children with SEN

Number of 2 year old funded children

Number of 3 year old funded children

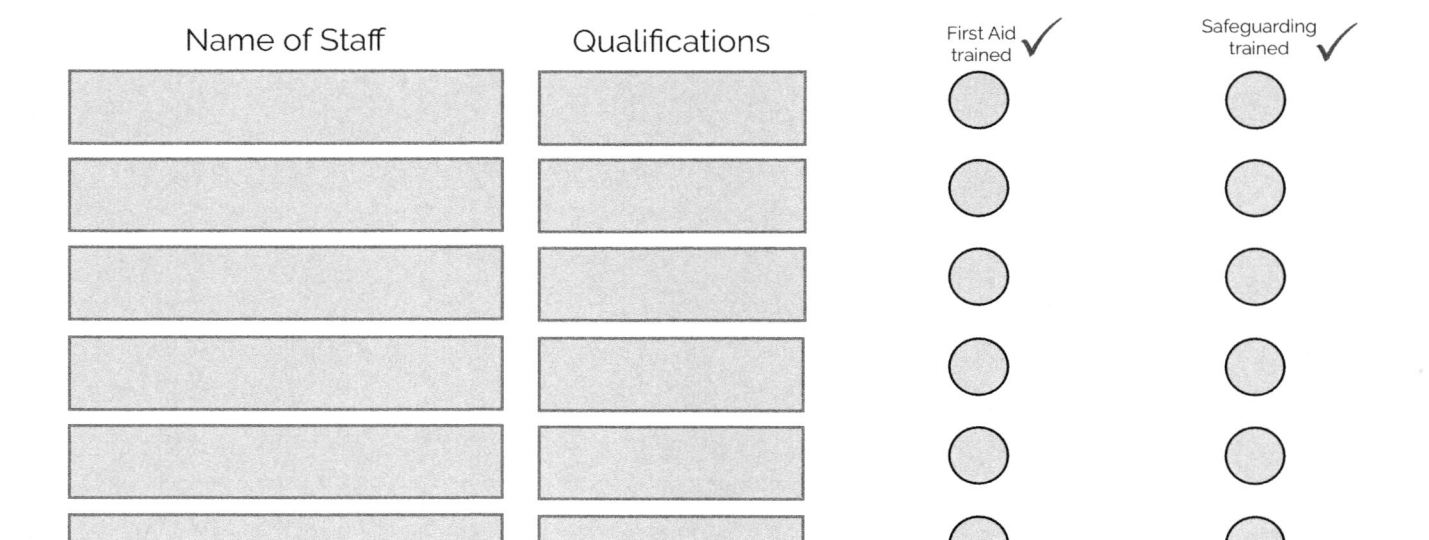

Staffing

Name of Staff	Qualifications	First Aid trained ✓	Safeguarding trained ✓

Jigsaw
EARLY YEARS CONSULTANCY

Date

Name of room	Age of room	Ratio in room
		:

Number of children in today	Number of children with EAL	Number of children with SEN	Number of 2 year old funded children	Number of 3 year old funded children

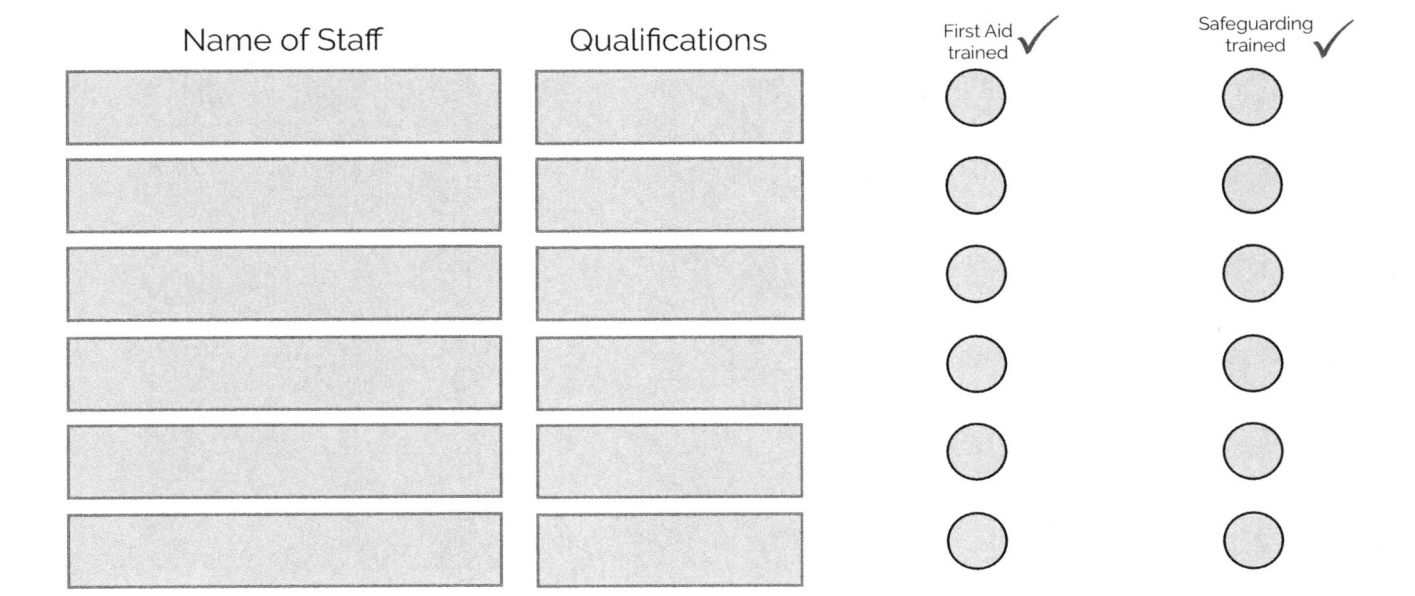

Staffing

Name of Staff	Qualifications	First Aid trained ✓	Safeguarding trained ✓
		○	○
		○	○
		○	○
		○	○
		○	○
		○	○

Jigsaw
EARLY YEARS CONSULTANCY

Date

Name of room	Age of room	Ratio in room
		:

Number of children in today	Number of children with EAL	Number of children with SEN	Number of 2 year old funded children	Number of 3 year old funded children

Staffing

Name of Staff	Qualifications	First Aid trained ✓	Safeguarding trained ✓
		○	○
		○	○
		○	○
		○	○
		○	○
		○	○

Date

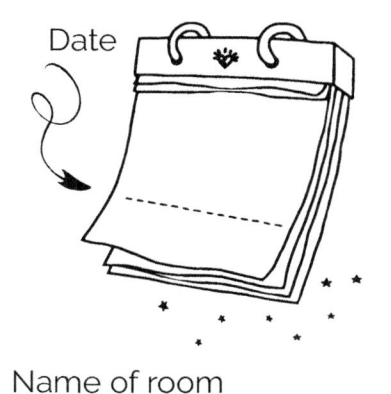

Name of room

Age of room

Ratio in room

:

Number of children in today	Number of children with EAL	Number of children with SEN	Number of 2 year old funded children	Number of 3 year old funded children

Staffing

Name of Staff	Qualifications	First Aid trained ✓	Safeguarding trained ✓

Jigsaw Early Years Consultancy

Date

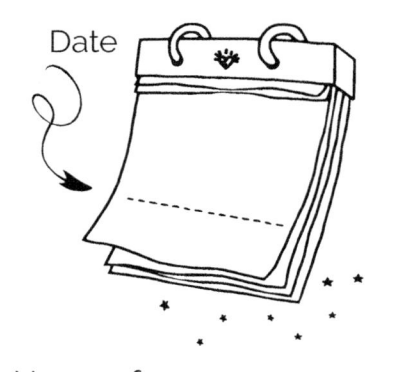

Name of room	Age of room	Ratio in room
		:

Number of children in today	Number of children with EAL	Number of children with SEN	Number of 2 year old funded children	Number of 3 year old funded children

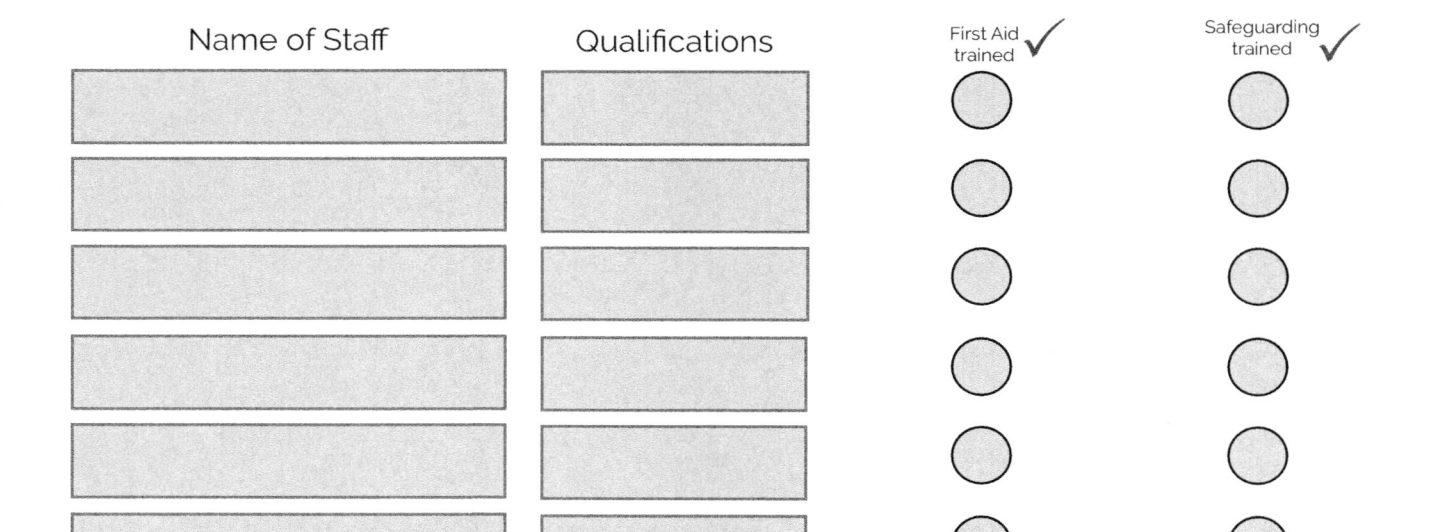

Staffing

Name of Staff	Qualifications	First Aid trained ✓	Safeguarding trained ✓
		○	○
		○	○
		○	○
		○	○
		○	○
		○	○

Date

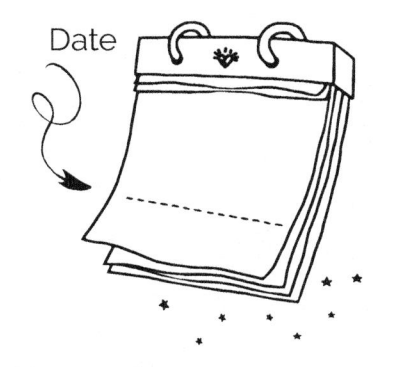

Jigsaw
EARLY YEARS CONSULTANCY

Name of room	Age of room	Ratio in room
		:

Number of children in today	Number of children with EAL	Number of children with SEN	Number of 2 year old funded children	Number of 3 year old funded children

Staffing

Name of Staff	Qualifications	First Aid trained ✓	Safeguarding trained ✓
		○	○
		○	○
		○	○
		○	○
		○	○
		○	○

Jigsaw
EARLY YEARS CONSULTANCY

Date

Name of room	Age of room	Ratio in room
		:

Number of children in today	Number of children with EAL	Number of children with SEN	Number of 2 year old funded children	Number of 3 year old funded children

Staffing

Name of Staff	Qualifications	First Aid trained ✓	Safeguarding trained ✓
		○	○
		○	○
		○	○
		○	○
		○	○
		○	○

Date

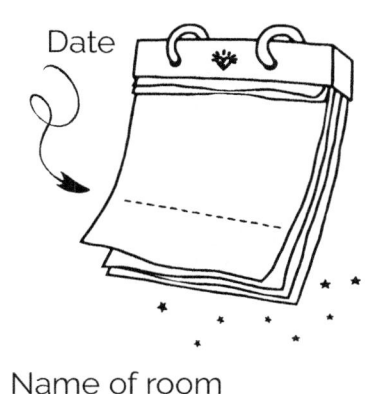

Name of room

Age of room

Ratio in room

:

Number of children in today

Number of children with EAL

Number of children with SEN

Number of 2 year old funded children

Number of 3 year old funded children

Staffing

Name of Staff	Qualifications	First Aid trained ✓	Safeguarding trained ✓

Date

Jigsaw
EARLY YEARS CONSULTANCY

Name of room	Age of room	Ratio in room
		:

Number of children in today	Number of children with EAL	Number of children with SEN	Number of 2 year old funded children	Number of 3 year old funded children

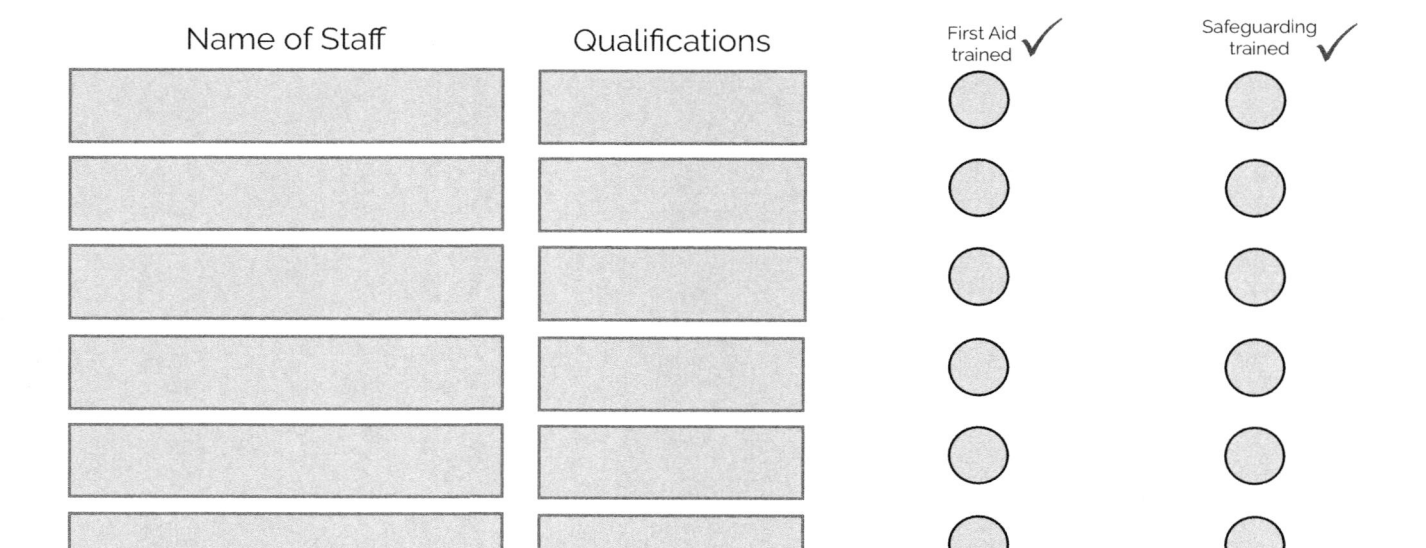

Staffing

Name of Staff	Qualifications	First Aid trained ✓	Safeguarding trained ✓
		○	○
		○	○
		○	○
		○	○
		○	○
		○	○

Jigsaw
EARLY YEARS CONSULTANCY

Date

Name of room

Age of room

Ratio in room

Number of children in today

Number of children with EAL

Number of children with SEN

Number of 2 year old funded children

Number of 3 year old funded children

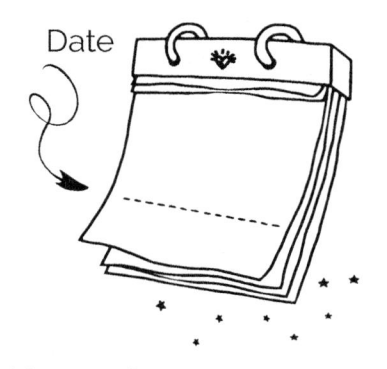

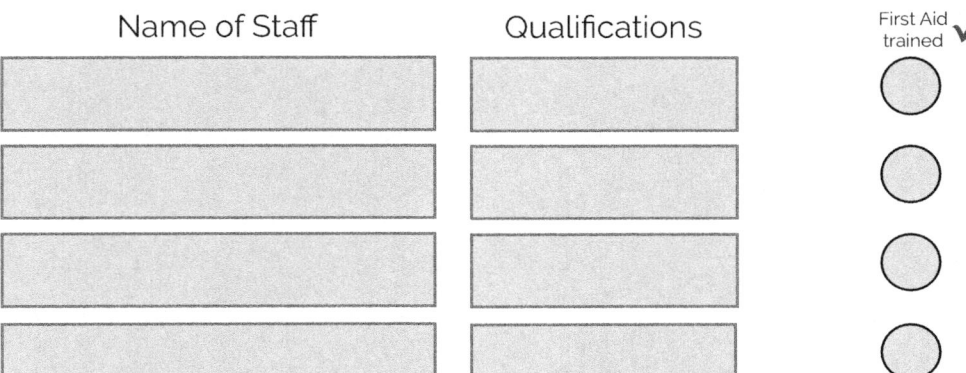

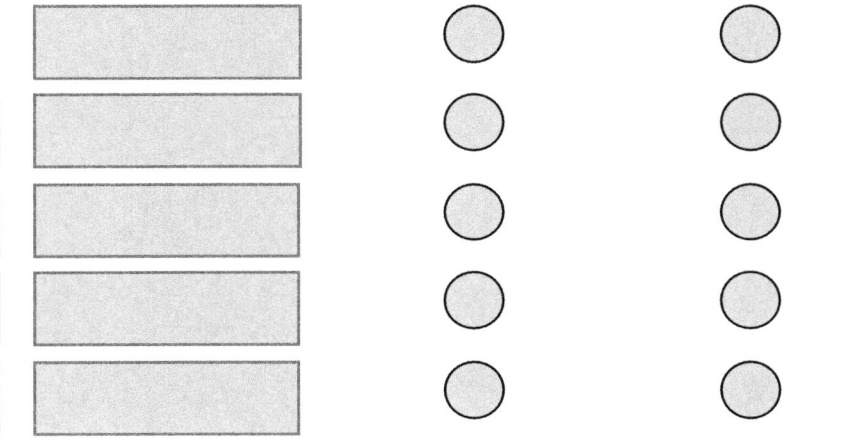

Staffing

Name of Staff	Qualifications	First Aid trained ✓	Safeguarding trained ✓

Date

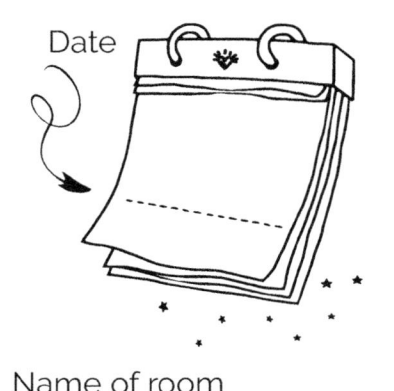

Name of room	Age of room	Ratio in room
		:

Number of children in today	Number of children with EAL	Number of children with SEN	Number of 2 year old funded children	Number of 3 year old funded children

Staffing

Name of Staff	Qualifications	First Aid trained ✓	Safeguarding trained ✓
		○	○
		○	○
		○	○
		○	○
		○	○
		○	○

Date

Name of room

Age of room

Ratio in room

:

Number of children in today

Number of children with EAL

Number of children with SEN

Number of 2 year old funded children

Number of 3 year old funded children

Staffing

Name of Staff	Qualifications	First Aid trained ✓	Safeguarding trained ✓

Jigsaw
EARLY YEARS CONSULTANCY

Date

Name of room	Age of room	Ratio in room
		:

Number of children in today	Number of children with EAL	Number of children with SEN	Number of 2 year old funded children	Number of 3 year old funded children

Staffing

Name of Staff	Qualifications	First Aid trained ✓	Safeguarding trained ✓
		○	○
		○	○
		○	○
		○	○
		○	○
		○	○

Date

Name of room

Age of room

Ratio in room

:

Number of children in today

Number of children with EAL

Number of children with SEN

Number of 2 year old funded children

Number of 3 year old funded children

Staffing

Name of Staff	Qualifications	First Aid trained ✓	Safeguarding trained ✓
		○	○
		○	○
		○	○
		○	○
		○	○
		○	○

Jigsaw
EARLY YEARS CONSULTANCY

Date

Name of room	Age of room	Ratio in room
		:

Number of children in today	Number of children with EAL	Number of children with SEN	Number of 2 year old funded children	Number of 3 year old funded children

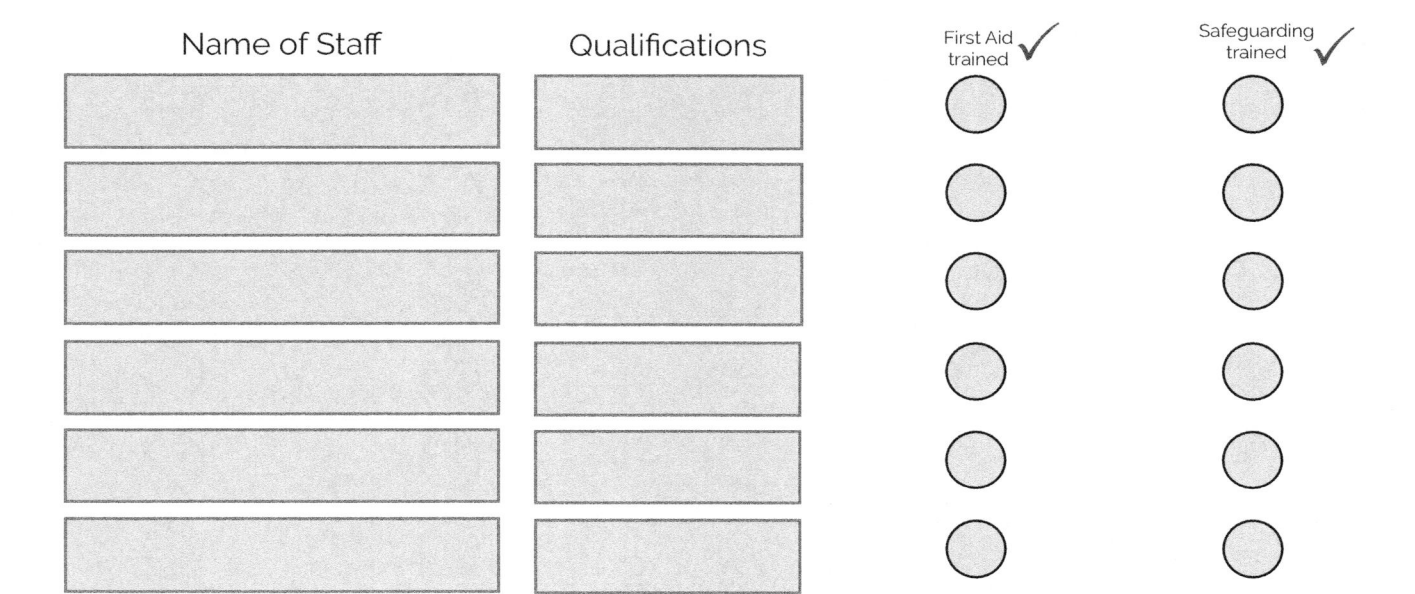

Staffing

Name of Staff	Qualifications	First Aid trained ✓	Safeguarding trained ✓
		○	○
		○	○
		○	○
		○	○
		○	○
		○	○

Jigsaw
EARLY YEARS CONSULTANCY

Date

Name of room

Age of room

Ratio in room

Number of children in today	Number of children with EAL	Number of children with SEN	Number of 2 year old funded children	Number of 3 year old funded children

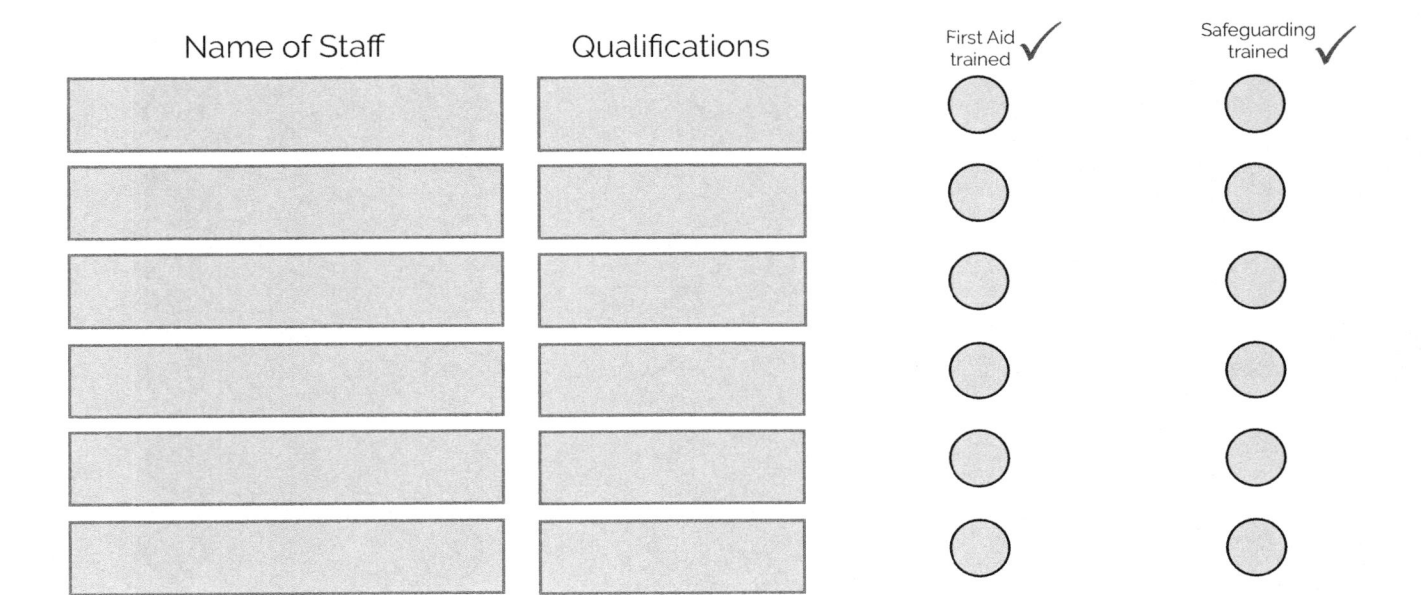

Staffing

Name of Staff	Qualifications	First Aid trained ✓	Safeguarding trained ✓

Jigsaw
EARLY YEARS CONSULTANCY

Date

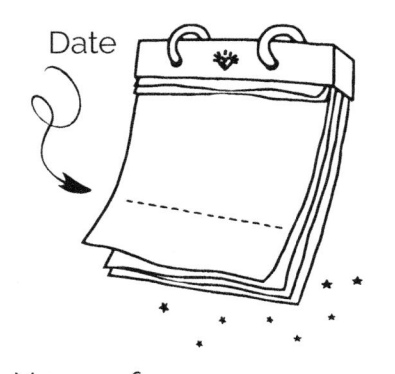

Name of room	Age of room	Ratio in room
		:

Number of children in today	Number of children with EAL	Number of children with SEN	Number of 2 year old funded children	Number of 3 year old funded children

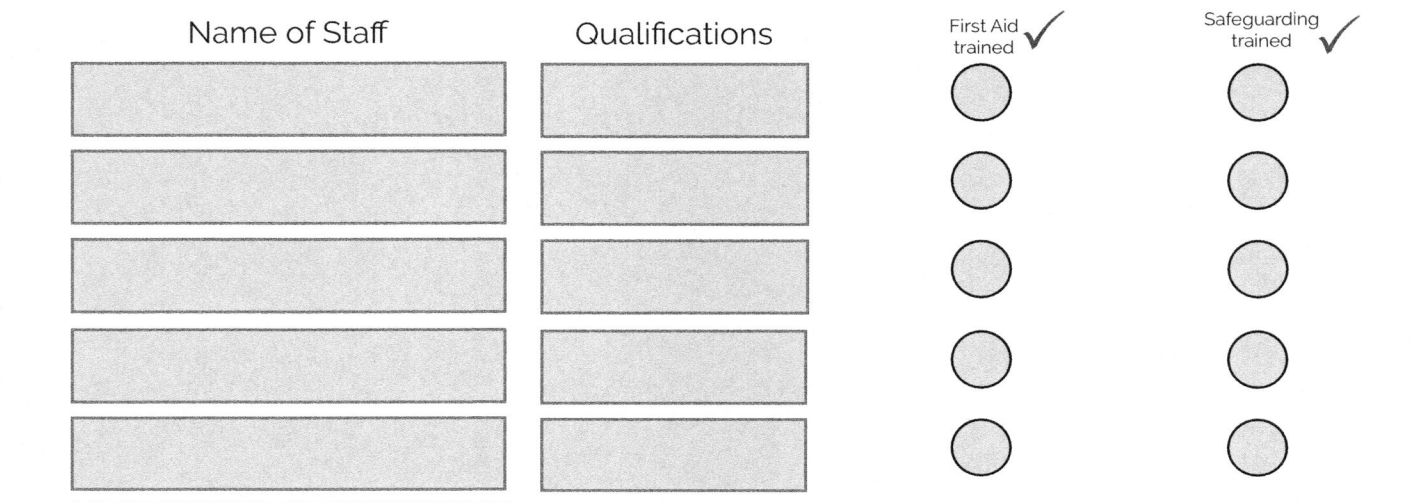

Staffing

Name of Staff	Qualifications	First Aid trained ✓	Safeguarding trained ✓
		○	○
		○	○
		○	○
		○	○
		○	○
		○	○

Jigsaw
EARLY YEARS CONSULTANCY

Date

Name of room	Age of room	Ratio in room
		:

Number of children in today	Number of children with EAL	Number of children with SEN	Number of 2 year old funded children	Number of 3 year old funded children

Staffing

Name of Staff	Qualifications	First Aid trained ✓	Safeguarding trained ✓
		○	○
		○	○
		○	○
		○	○
		○	○
		○	○

Jigsaw
EARLY YEARS CONSULTANCY

Date

Name of room	Age of room	Ratio in room
		:

Number of children in today	Number of children with EAL	Number of children with SEN	Number of 2 year old funded children	Number of 3 year old funded children

Staffing

Name of Staff	Qualifications	First Aid trained ✓	Safeguarding trained ✓
		○	○
		○	○
		○	○
		○	○
		○	○
		○	○

Date

Name of room

Age of room

Ratio in room

:

Number of children in today

Number of children with EAL

Number of children with SEN

Number of 2 year old funded children

Number of 3 year old funded children

Staffing

Name of Staff	Qualifications	First Aid trained ✓	Safeguarding trained ✓

Jigsaw
EARLY YEARS CONSULTANCY

Date

Name of room

Age of room

Ratio in room

Number of children in today	Number of children with EAL	Number of children with SEN	Number of 2 year old funded children	Number of 3 year old funded children

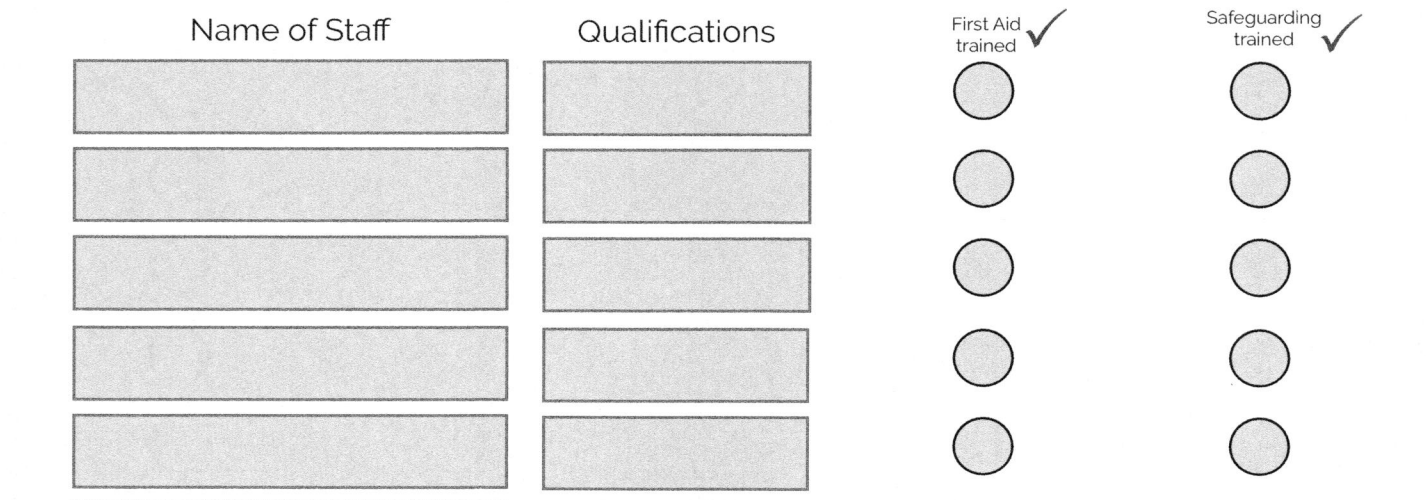

Staffing

Name of Staff	Qualifications	First Aid trained ✓	Safeguarding trained ✓

Date

Jigsaw
EARLY YEARS CONSULTANCY

Name of room	Age of room	Ratio in room
		:

Number of children in today	Number of children with EAL	Number of children with SEN	Number of 2 year old funded children	Number of 3 year old funded children

Staffing

Name of Staff	Qualifications	First Aid trained ✓	Safeguarding trained ✓
		○	○
		○	○
		○	○
		○	○
		○	○
		○	○

Jigsaw
EARLY YEARS CONSULTANCY

Date

Name of room	Age of room	Ratio in room
		:

Number of children in today	Number of children with EAL	Number of children with SEN	Number of 2 year old funded children	Number of 3 year old funded children

Staffing

Name of Staff	Qualifications	First Aid trained ✓	Safeguarding trained ✓
		◯	◯
		◯	◯
		◯	◯
		◯	◯
		◯	◯
		◯	◯

Jigsaw
EARLY YEARS CONSULTANCY

Date

Name of room

Age of room

Ratio in room
:

Number of children in today

Number of children with EAL

Number of children with SEN

Number of 2 year old funded children

Number of 3 year old funded children

Staffing

Name of Staff	Qualifications	First Aid trained ✓	Safeguarding trained ✓
		○	○
		○	○
		○	○
		○	○
		○	○
		○	○

Date

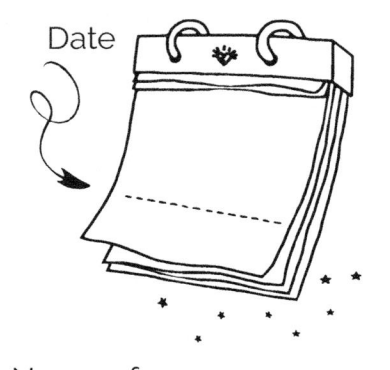

Name of room

Age of room

Ratio in room

| | : | |

Number of children in today

Number of children with EAL

Number of children with SEN

Number of 2 year old funded children

Number of 3 year old funded children

Staffing

Name of Staff	Qualifications	First Aid trained ✓	Safeguarding trained ✓
		◯	◯
		◯	◯
		◯	◯
		◯	◯
		◯	◯
		◯	◯

Jigsaw
EARLY YEARS CONSULTANCY

Date

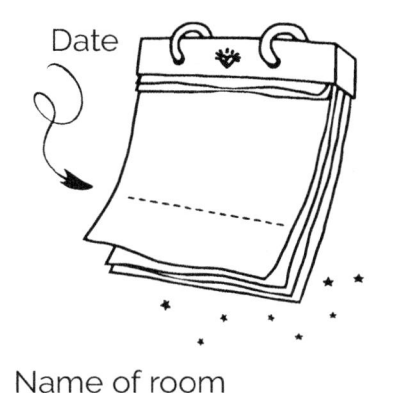

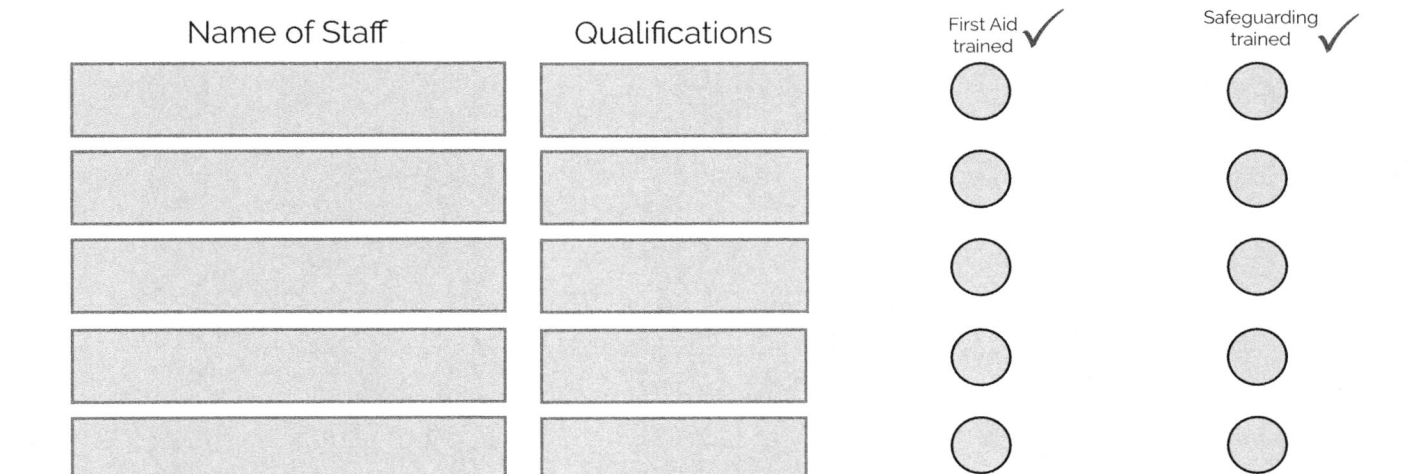

Name of room	Age of room	Ratio in room
		:

Number of children in today	Number of children with EAL	Number of children with SEN	Number of 2 year old funded children	Number of 3 year old funded children

Staffing

Name of Staff	Qualifications	First Aid trained ✓	Safeguarding trained ✓
		◯	◯
		◯	◯
		◯	◯
		◯	◯
		◯	◯
		◯	◯

Jigsaw
EARLY YEARS CONSULTANCY

Date

Name of room

Age of room

Ratio in room

Number of children in today	Number of children with EAL	Number of children with SEN	Number of 2 year old funded children	Number of 3 year old funded children

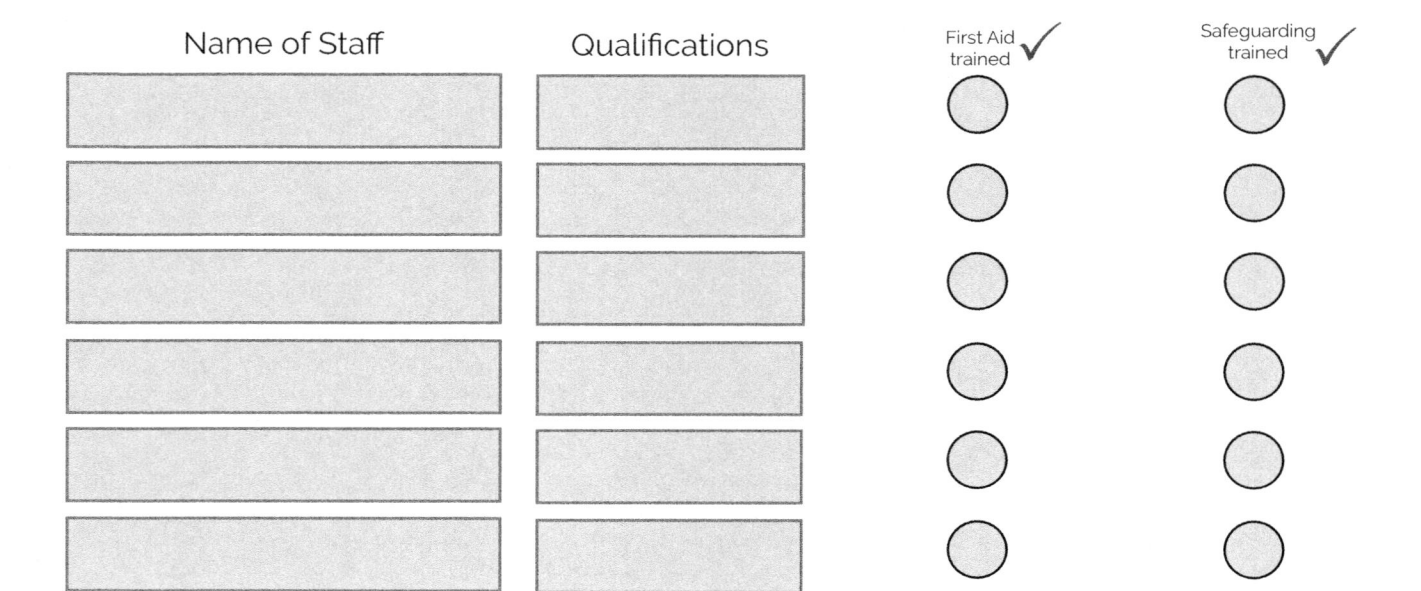

Staffing

Name of Staff	Qualifications	First Aid trained ✓	Safeguarding trained ✓
		◯	◯
		◯	◯
		◯	◯
		◯	◯
		◯	◯
		◯	◯

Jigsaw
EARLY YEARS CONSULTANCY

Date

Name of room	Age of room	Ratio in room
		:

Number of children in today	Number of children with EAL	Number of children with SEN	Number of 2 year old funded children	Number of 3 year old funded children

Staffing

Name of Staff	Qualifications	First Aid trained ✓	Safeguarding trained ✓
		◯	◯
		◯	◯
		◯	◯
		◯	◯
		◯	◯
		◯	◯

Jigsaw
EARLY YEARS CONSULTANCY

Date

Name of room	Age of room	Ratio in room
		:

Number of children in today	Number of children with EAL	Number of children with SEN	Number of 2 year old funded children	Number of 3 year old funded children

Staffing

Name of Staff	Qualifications	First Aid trained ✓	Safeguarding trained ✓
		○	○
		○	○
		○	○
		○	○
		○	○
		○	○

Date

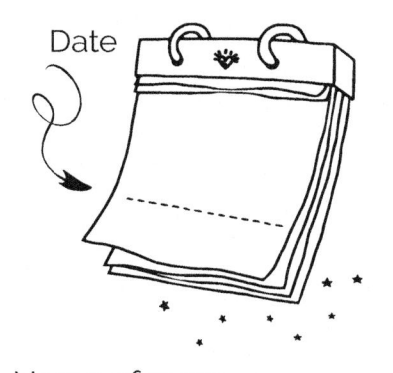

Jigsaw
EARLY YEARS CONSULTANCY

Name of room

Age of room

Ratio in room
:

Number of children in today

Number of children with EAL

Number of children with SEN

Number of 2 year old funded children

Number of 3 year old funded children

Staffing

Name of Staff	Qualifications	First Aid trained ✓	Safeguarding trained ✓
		○	○
		○	○
		○	○
		○	○
		○	○
		○	○

Date

Name of room

Age of room

Ratio in room

:

Number of children in today	Number of children with EAL	Number of children with SEN	Number of 2 year old funded children	Number of 3 year old funded children

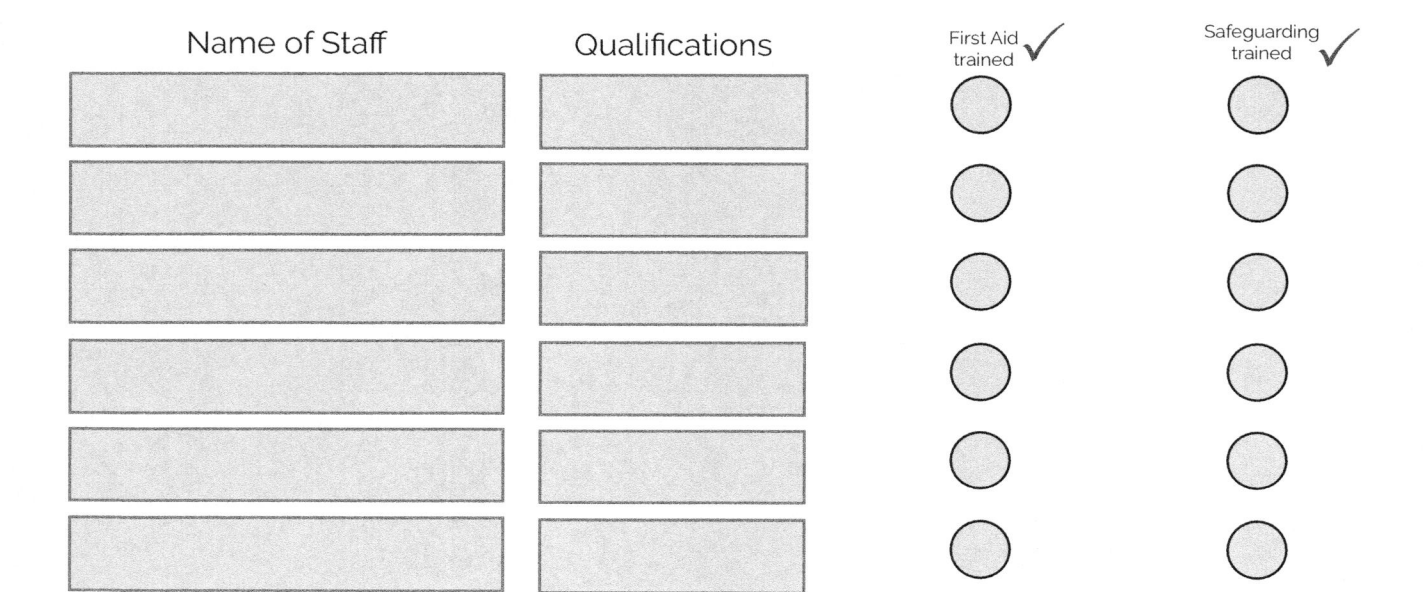

Staffing

Name of Staff	Qualifications	First Aid trained ✓	Safeguarding trained ✓

Jigsaw
EARLY YEARS CONSULTANCY

Date

Name of room

Age of room

Ratio in room

:

Number of children in today

Number of children with EAL

Number of children with SEN

Number of 2 year old funded children

Number of 3 year old funded children

Staffing

Name of Staff	Qualifications	First Aid trained ✓	Safeguarding trained ✓
		○	○
		○	○
		○	○
		○	○
		○	○
		○	○

Jigsaw
EARLY YEARS CONSULTANCY

Date

Name of room	Age of room	Ratio in room
		:

Number of children in today	Number of children with EAL	Number of children with SEN	Number of 2 year old funded children	Number of 3 year old funded children

Staffing

Name of Staff	Qualifications	First Aid trained ✓	Safeguarding trained ✓
		○	○
		○	○
		○	○
		○	○
		○	○
		○	○

Jigsaw
EARLY YEARS CONSULTANCY

Date

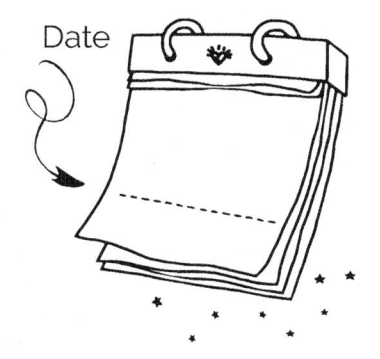

Name of room	Age of room	Ratio in room
		:

Number of children in today	Number of children with EAL	Number of children with SEN	Number of 2 year old funded children	Number of 3 year old funded children

Staffing

Name of Staff	Qualifications	First Aid trained ✓	Safeguarding trained ✓
		◯	◯
		◯	◯
		◯	◯
		◯	◯
		◯	◯
		◯	◯

Jigsaw
EARLY YEARS CONSULTANCY

Date

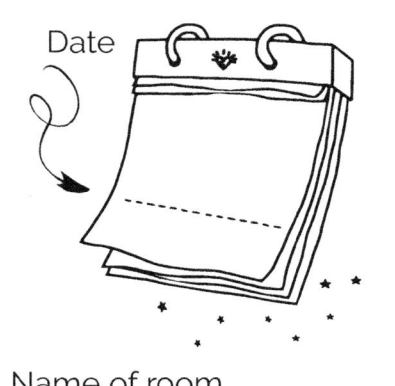

Name of room

Age of room

Ratio in room

Number of children in today

Number of children with EAL

Number of children with SEN

Number of 2 year old funded children

Number of 3 year old funded children

Staffing

Name of Staff	Qualifications	First Aid trained ✓	Safeguarding trained ✓

Jigsaw
EARLY YEARS CONSULTANCY

Date

Name of room

Age of room

Ratio in room

:

Number of children in today	Number of children with EAL	Number of children with SEN	Number of 2 year old funded children	Number of 3 year old funded children

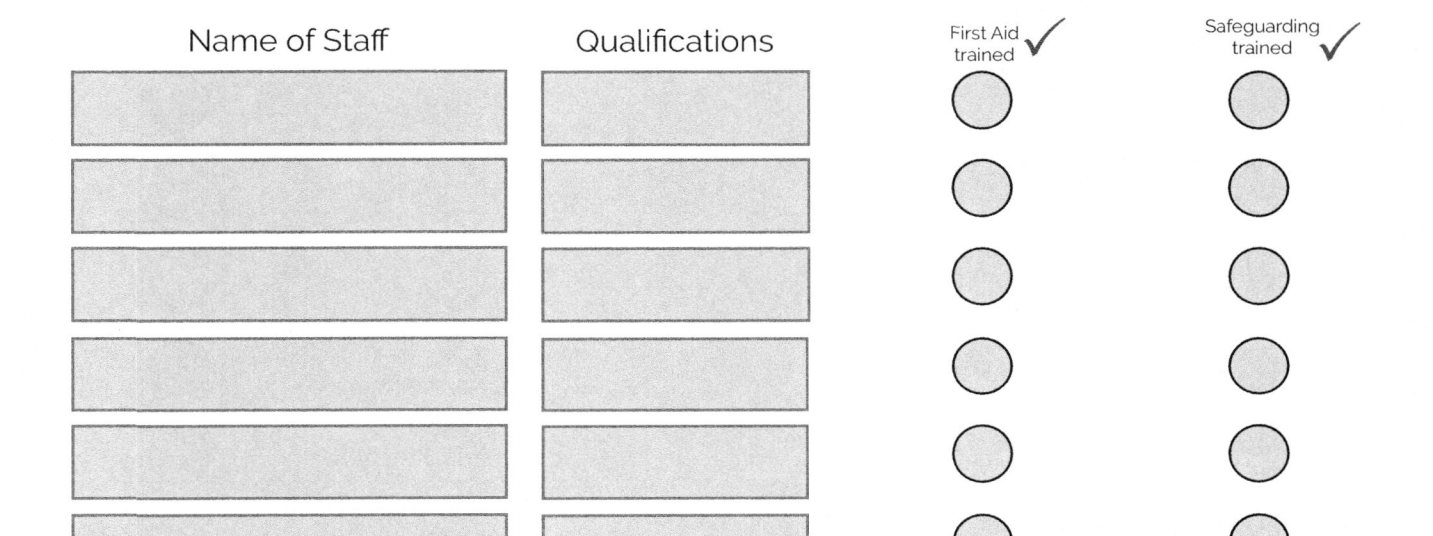

Staffing

Name of Staff	Qualifications	First Aid trained ✓	Safeguarding trained ✓
		○	○
		○	○
		○	○
		○	○
		○	○
		○	○

Date

Name of room	Age of room	Ratio in room
		:

Number of children in today	Number of children with EAL	Number of children with SEN	Number of 2 year old funded children	Number of 3 year old funded children

Staffing

Name of Staff	Qualifications	First Aid trained ✓	Safeguarding trained ✓

Date

Jigsaw
EARLY YEARS CONSULTANCY

Name of room	Age of room	Ratio in room
		:

Number of children in today	Number of children with EAL	Number of children with SEN	Number of 2 year old funded children	Number of 3 year old funded children

Staffing

Name of Staff	Qualifications	First Aid trained ✓	Safeguarding trained ✓
		◯	◯
		◯	◯
		◯	◯
		◯	◯
		◯	◯
		◯	◯

Jigsaw
EARLY YEARS CONSULTANCY

Date

Name of room	Age of room	Ratio in room
		:

Number of children in today	Number of children with EAL	Number of children with SEN	Number of 2 year old funded children	Number of 3 year old funded children

Staffing

Name of Staff	Qualifications	First Aid trained ✓	Safeguarding trained ✓
		◯	◯
		◯	◯
		◯	◯
		◯	◯
		◯	◯
		◯	◯

Jigsaw Early Years Consultancy

Date

Name of room	Age of room	Ratio in room
		:

Number of children in today	Number of children with EAL	Number of children with SEN	Number of 2 year old funded children	Number of 3 year old funded children

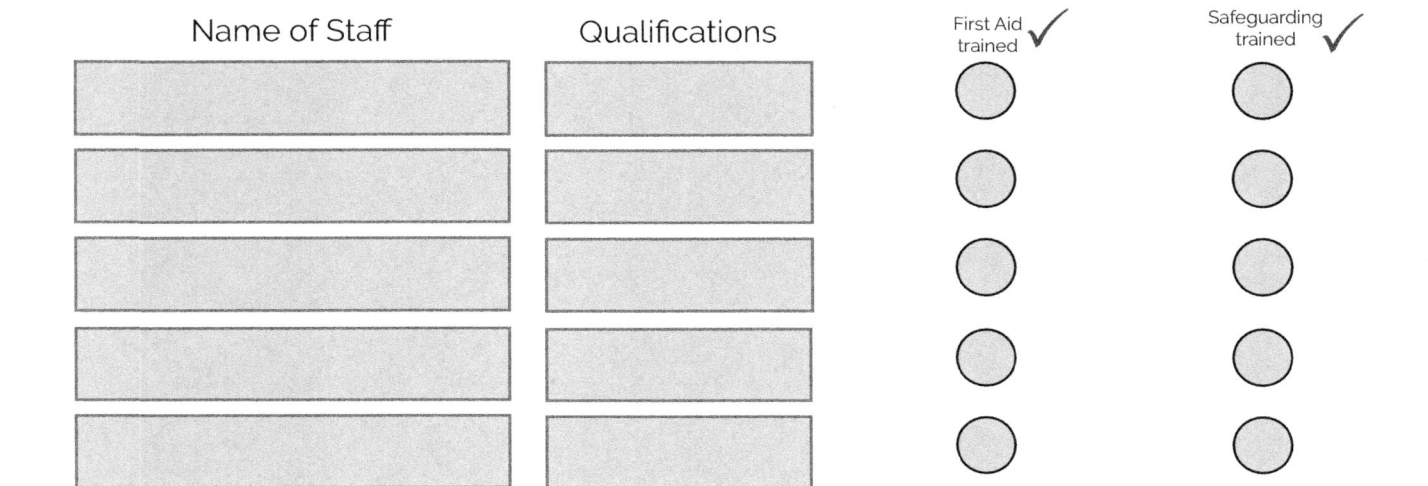

Staffing

Name of Staff	Qualifications	First Aid trained ✓	Safeguarding trained ✓
		◯	◯
		◯	◯
		◯	◯
		◯	◯
		◯	◯
		◯	◯

Jigsaw
EARLY YEARS CONSULTANCY

Date

Name of room	Age of room	Ratio in room
		:

Number of children in today	Number of children with EAL	Number of children with SEN	Number of 2 year old funded children	Number of 3 year old funded children

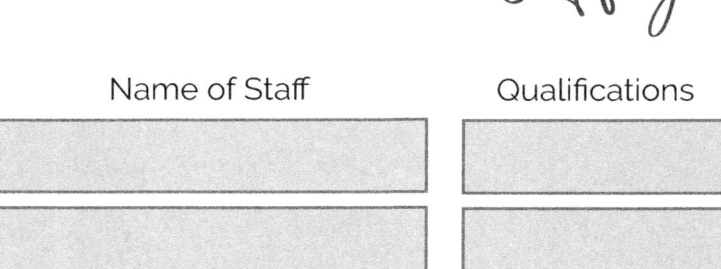

Staffing

Name of Staff	Qualifications	First Aid trained ✓	Safeguarding trained ✓
		○	○
		○	○
		○	○
		○	○
		○	○
		○	○

Date

Jigsaw
EARLY YEARS CONSULTANCY

Name of room	Age of room	Ratio in room
		:

Number of children in today	Number of children with EAL	Number of children with SEN	Number of 2 year old funded children	Number of 3 year old funded children

Staffing

Name of Staff	Qualifications	First Aid trained ✓	Safeguarding trained ✓
		○	○
		○	○
		○	○
		○	○
		○	○
		○	○

Date

Name of room

Age of room

Ratio in room

:

Number of children in today

Number of children with EAL

Number of children with SEN

Number of 2 year old funded children

Number of 3 year old funded children

Staffing

Name of Staff	Qualifications	First Aid trained ✓	Safeguarding trained ✓
		○	○
		○	○
		○	○
		○	○
		○	○
		○	○

Date

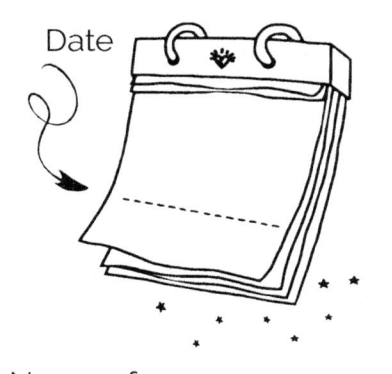

Name of room	Age of room	Ratio in room
		:

Number of children in today	Number of children with EAL	Number of children with SEN	Number of 2 year old funded children	Number of 3 year old funded children

Staffing

Name of Staff	Qualifications	First Aid trained ✓	Safeguarding trained ✓
		○	○
		○	○
		○	○
		○	○
		○	○
		○	○

Date

Name of room

Age of room

Ratio in room

:

Number of children in today	Number of children with EAL	Number of children with SEN	Number of 2 year old funded children	Number of 3 year old funded children

Staffing

Name of Staff	Qualifications	First Aid trained ✓	Safeguarding trained ✓
		○	○
		○	○
		○	○
		○	○
		○	○
		○	○

Jigsaw
EARLY YEARS CONSULTANCY

Date

Name of room

Age of room

Ratio in room

Number of children in today

Number of children with EAL

Number of children with SEN

Number of 2 year old funded children

Number of 3 year old funded children

Staffing

Name of Staff	Qualifications	First Aid trained ✓	Safeguarding trained ✓

Jigsaw
EARLY YEARS CONSULTANCY

Date

Name of room

Age of room

Ratio in room

:

Number of children in today

Number of children with EAL

Number of children with SEN

Number of 2 year old funded children

Number of 3 year old funded children

Staffing

Name of Staff	Qualifications	First Aid trained ✓	Safeguarding trained ✓

Jigsaw
EARLY YEARS CONSULTANCY

Date

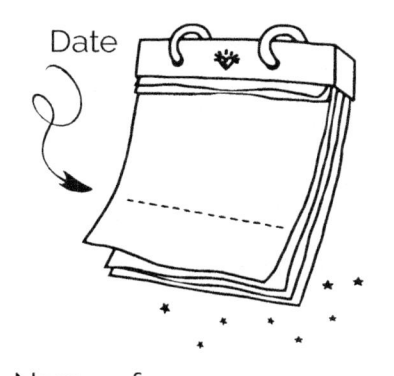

Name of room	Age of room	Ratio in room
		:

Number of children in today	Number of children with EAL	Number of children with SEN	Number of 2 year old funded children	Number of 3 year old funded children

Staffing

Name of Staff	Qualifications	First Aid trained ✓	Safeguarding trained ✓
		○	○
		○	○
		○	○
		○	○
		○	○
		○	○

Date

Name of room	Age of room	Ratio in room
		:

Number of children in today	Number of children with EAL	Number of children with SEN	Number of 2 year old funded children	Number of 3 year old funded children

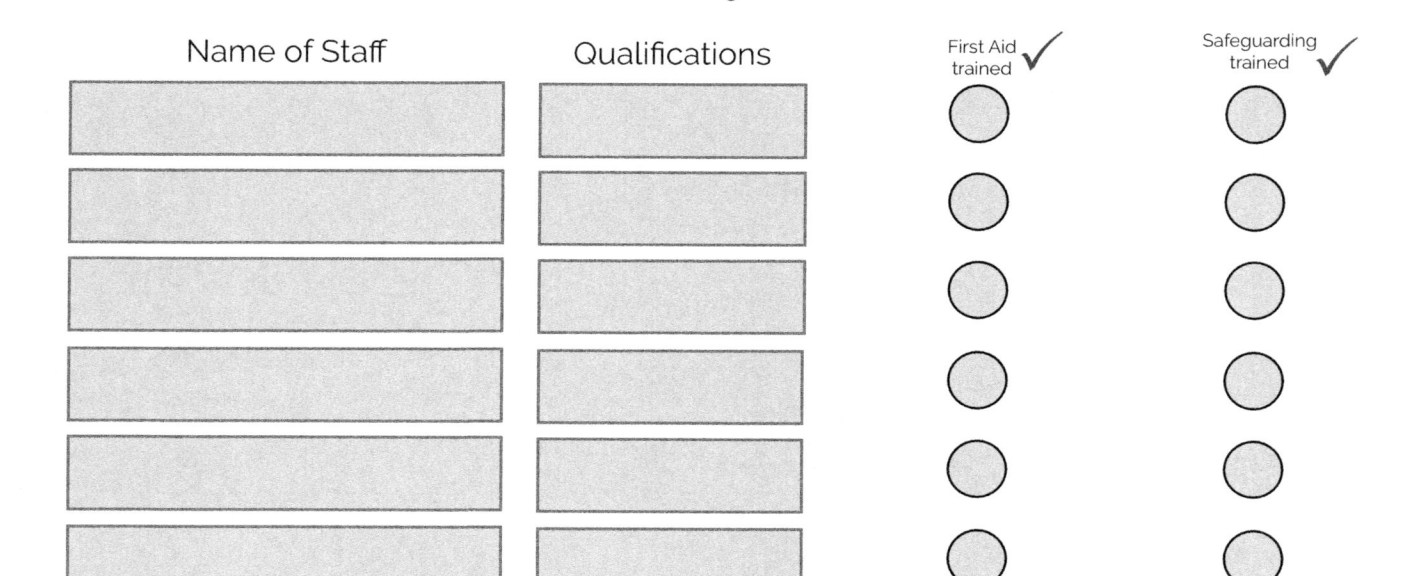

Staffing

Name of Staff	Qualifications	First Aid trained ✓	Safeguarding trained ✓

Jigsaw
EARLY YEARS CONSULTANCY

Date

Name of room	Age of room	Ratio in room
		:

Number of children in today	Number of children with EAL	Number of children with SEN	Number of 2 year old funded children	Number of 3 year old funded children

Staffing

Name of Staff	Qualifications	First Aid trained ✓	Safeguarding trained ✓
		○	○
		○	○
		○	○
		○	○
		○	○
		○	○

Jigsaw
EARLY YEARS CONSULTANCY

Date

Name of room

Age of room

Ratio in room

:

Number of children in today

Number of children with EAL

Number of children with SEN

Number of 2 year old funded children

Number of 3 year old funded children

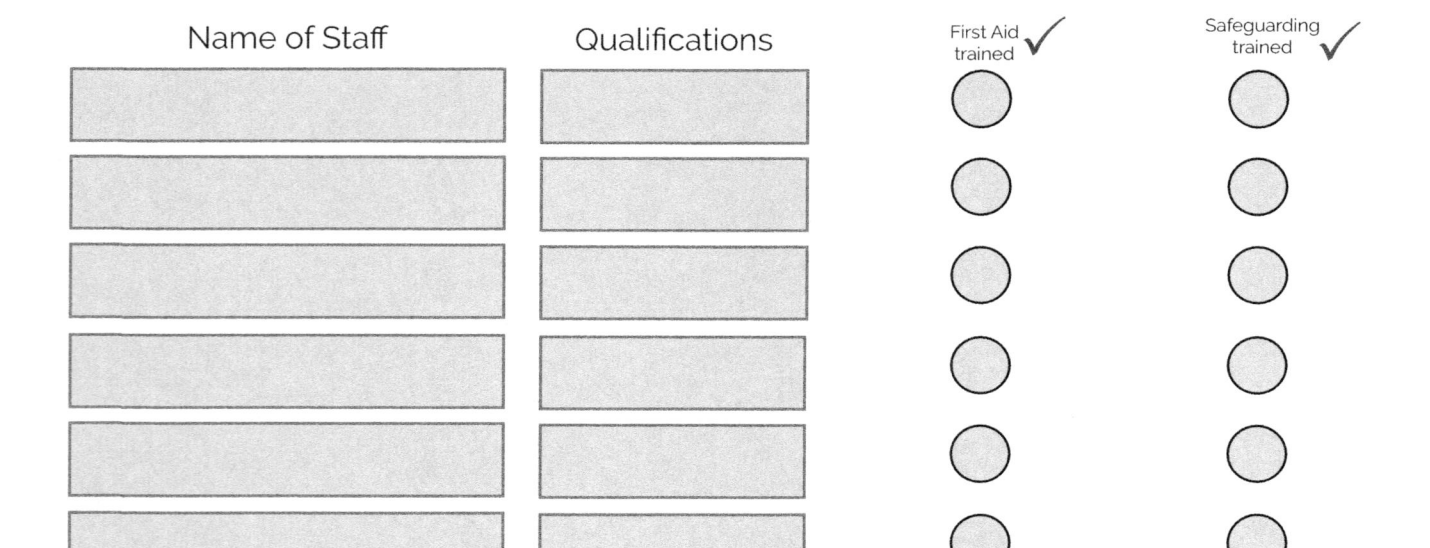

Staffing

Name of Staff	Qualifications	First Aid trained ✓	Safeguarding trained ✓

Jigsaw
EARLY YEARS CONSULTANCY

Date

Name of room	Age of room	Ratio in room
		:

Number of children in today	Number of children with EAL	Number of children with SEN	Number of 2 year old funded children	Number of 3 year old funded children

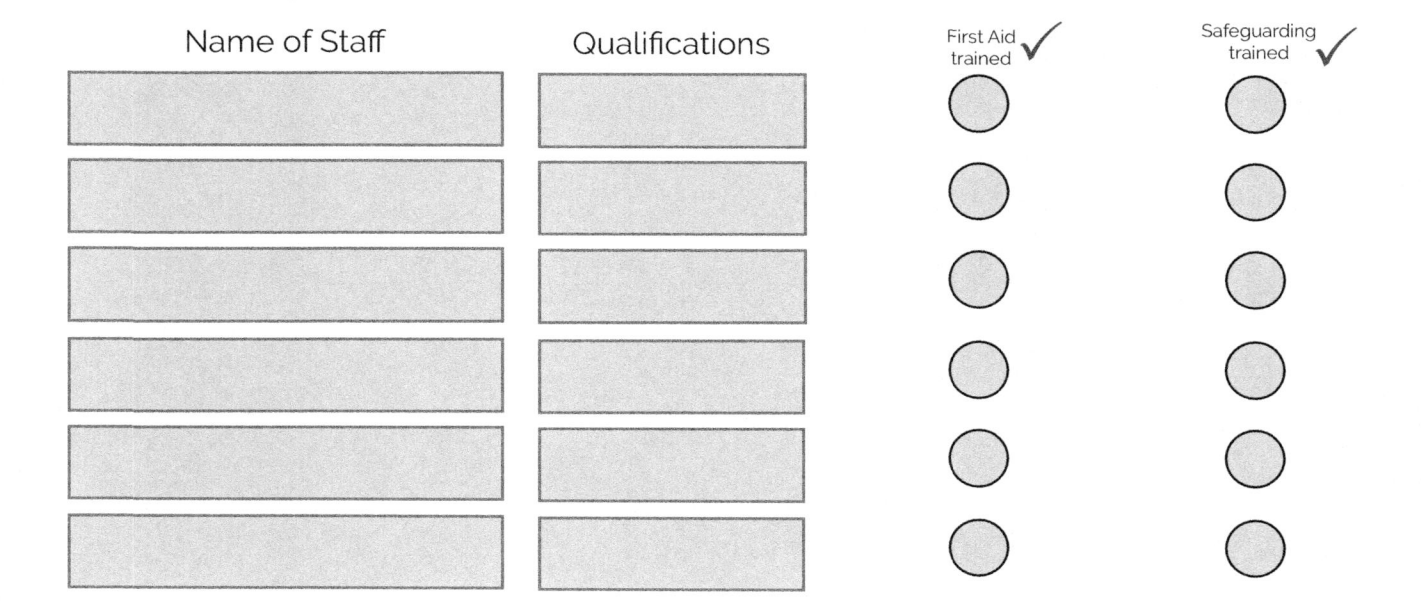

Staffing

Name of Staff	Qualifications	First Aid trained ✓	Safeguarding trained ✓

Date

Jigsaw
EARLY YEARS CONSULTANCY

Name of room

Age of room

Ratio in room

:

Number of children in today

Number of children with EAL

Number of children with SEN

Number of 2 year old funded children

Number of 3 year old funded children

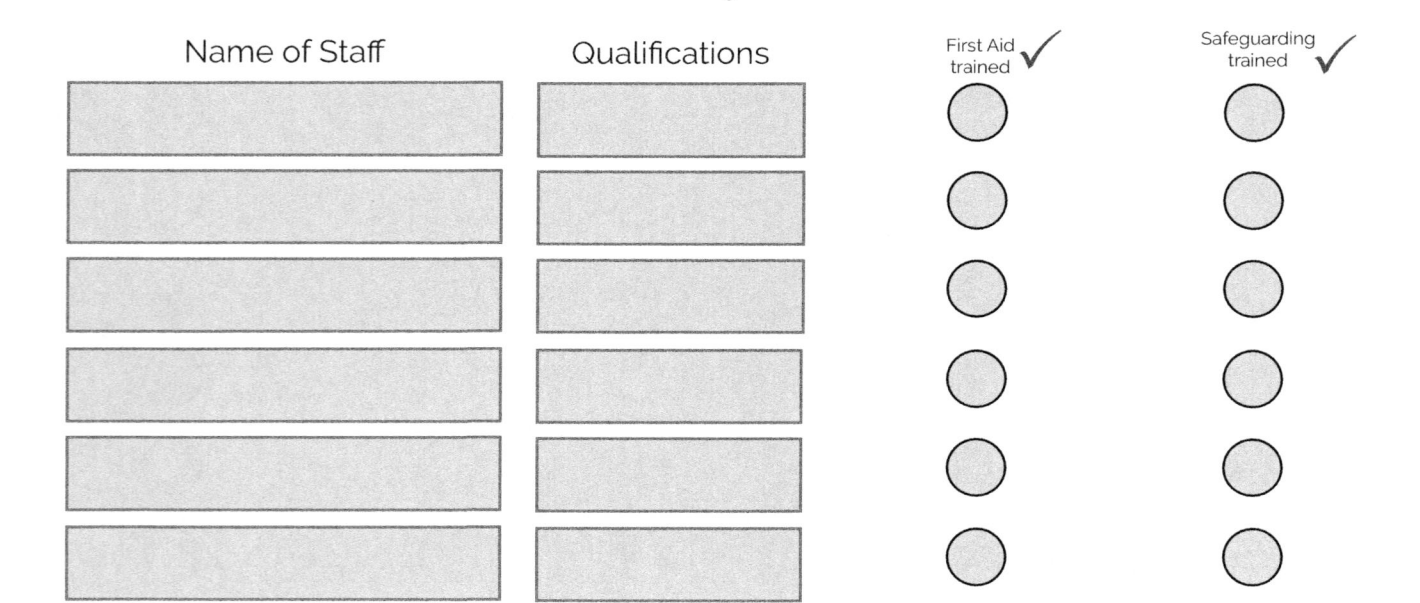

Staffing

Name of Staff	Qualifications	First Aid trained ✓	Safeguarding trained ✓
		○	○
		○	○
		○	○
		○	○
		○	○
		○	○

Date

Name of room	Age of room	Ratio in room
		:

Number of children in today	Number of children with EAL	Number of children with SEN	Number of 2 year old funded children	Number of 3 year old funded children

Staffing

Name of Staff	Qualifications	First Aid trained ✓	Safeguarding trained ✓
		○	○
		○	○
		○	○
		○	○
		○	○
		○	○

Date

Name of room

Age of room

Ratio in room

:

Number of children in today

Number of children with EAL

Number of children with SEN

Number of 2 year old funded children

Number of 3 year old funded children

Staffing

Name of Staff	Qualifications	First Aid trained ✓	Safeguarding trained ✓
		○	○
		○	○
		○	○
		○	○
		○	○
		○	○

Jigsaw EARLY YEARS CONSULTANCY

Date

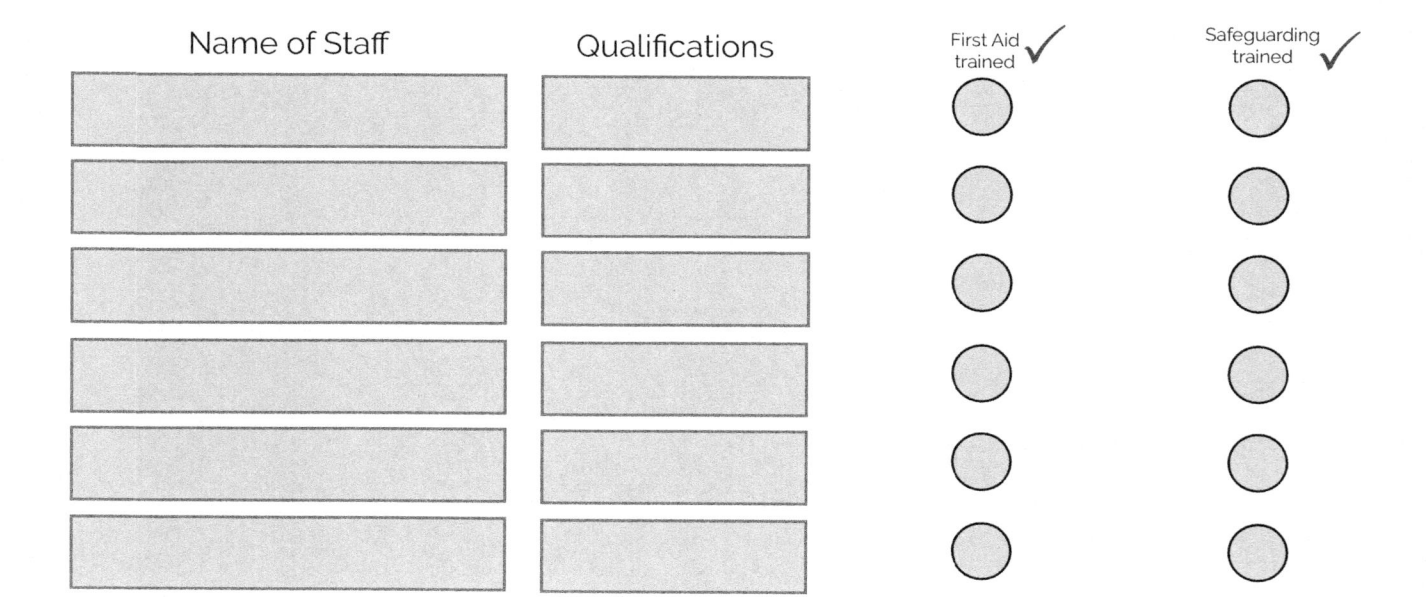

Name of room	Age of room	Ratio in room
		:

Number of children in today	Number of children with EAL	Number of children with SEN	Number of 2 year old funded children	Number of 3 year old funded children

Staffing

Name of Staff	Qualifications	First Aid trained ✓	Safeguarding trained ✓
		○	○
		○	○
		○	○
		○	○
		○	○
		○	○

Jigsaw
EARLY YEARS CONSULTANCY

Date

Name of room	Age of room	Ratio in room
		:

Number of children in today	Number of children with EAL	Number of children with SEN	Number of 2 year old funded children	Number of 3 year old funded children

Staffing

Name of Staff	Qualifications	First Aid trained ✓	Safeguarding trained ✓
		◯	◯
		◯	◯
		◯	◯
		◯	◯
		◯	◯
		◯	◯

Date

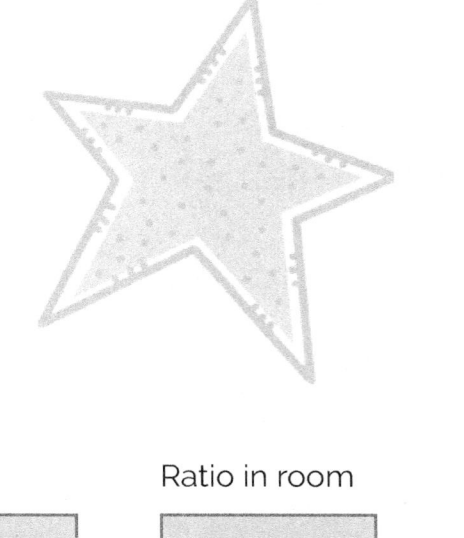

Name of room

Age of room

Ratio in room

:

Number of children in today

Number of children with EAL

Number of children with SEN

Number of 2 year old funded children

Number of 3 year old funded children

Staffing

Name of Staff	Qualifications	First Aid trained ✓	Safeguarding trained ✓
		○	○
		○	○
		○	○
		○	○
		○	○
		○	○

Date

Jigsaw
EARLY YEARS CONSULTANCY

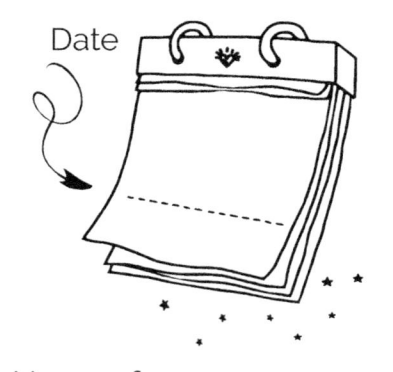

Name of room

Age of room

Ratio in room

:

Number of children in today

Number of children with EAL

Number of children with SEN

Number of 2 year old funded children

Number of 3 year old funded children

Staffing

Name of Staff	Qualifications	First Aid trained ✓	Safeguarding trained ✓
		○	○
		○	○
		○	○
		○	○
		○	○
		○	○

Jigsaw
EARLY YEARS CONSULTANCY

Date

Name of room	Age of room	Ratio in room
		:

Number of children in today	Number of children with EAL	Number of children with SEN	Number of 2 year old funded children	Number of 3 year old funded children

Staffing

Name of Staff	Qualifications	First Aid trained ✓	Safeguarding trained ✓
		○	○
		○	○
		○	○
		○	○
		○	○
		○	○

Jigsaw
EARLY YEARS CONSULTANCY

Date

Name of room	Age of room	Ratio in room
		:

Number of children in today	Number of children with EAL	Number of children with SEN	Number of 2 year old funded children	Number of 3 year old funded children

Staffing

Name of Staff	Qualifications	First Aid trained ✓	Safeguarding trained ✓
		○	○
		○	○
		○	○
		○	○
		○	○
		○	○

Jigsaw
EARLY YEARS CONSULTANCY

Date

Name of room	Age of room	Ratio in room
		:

Number of children in today	Number of children with EAL	Number of children with SEN	Number of 2 year old funded children	Number of 3 year old funded children

Staffing

Name of Staff	Qualifications	First Aid trained ✓	Safeguarding trained ✓
		○	○
		○	○
		○	○
		○	○
		○	○
		○	○

Jigsaw
EARLY YEARS CONSULTANCY

Date

Name of room	Age of room	Ratio in room
		:

Number of children in today	Number of children with EAL	Number of children with SEN	Number of 2 year old funded children	Number of 3 year old funded children

Staffing

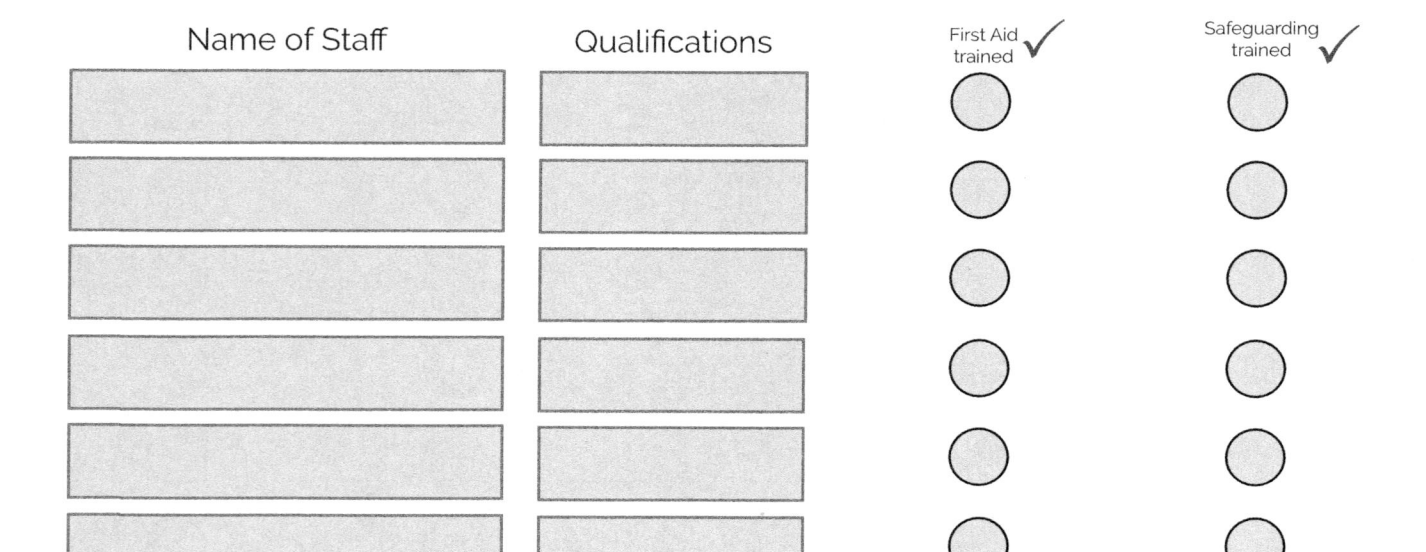

Name of Staff	Qualifications	First Aid trained ✓	Safeguarding trained ✓
		○	○
		○	○
		○	○
		○	○
		○	○
		○	○

Date

Jigsaw
EARLY YEARS CONSULTANCY

Name of room	Age of room	Ratio in room
		:

Number of children in today	Number of children with EAL	Number of children with SEN	Number of 2 year old funded children	Number of 3 year old funded children

Staffing

Name of Staff	Qualifications	First Aid trained ✓	Safeguarding trained ✓
		○	○
		○	○
		○	○
		○	○
		○	○
		○	○

Date

Jigsaw
EARLY YEARS CONSULTANCY

Name of room	Age of room	Ratio in room
		:

Number of children in today	Number of children with EAL	Number of children with SEN	Number of 2 year old funded children	Number of 3 year old funded children

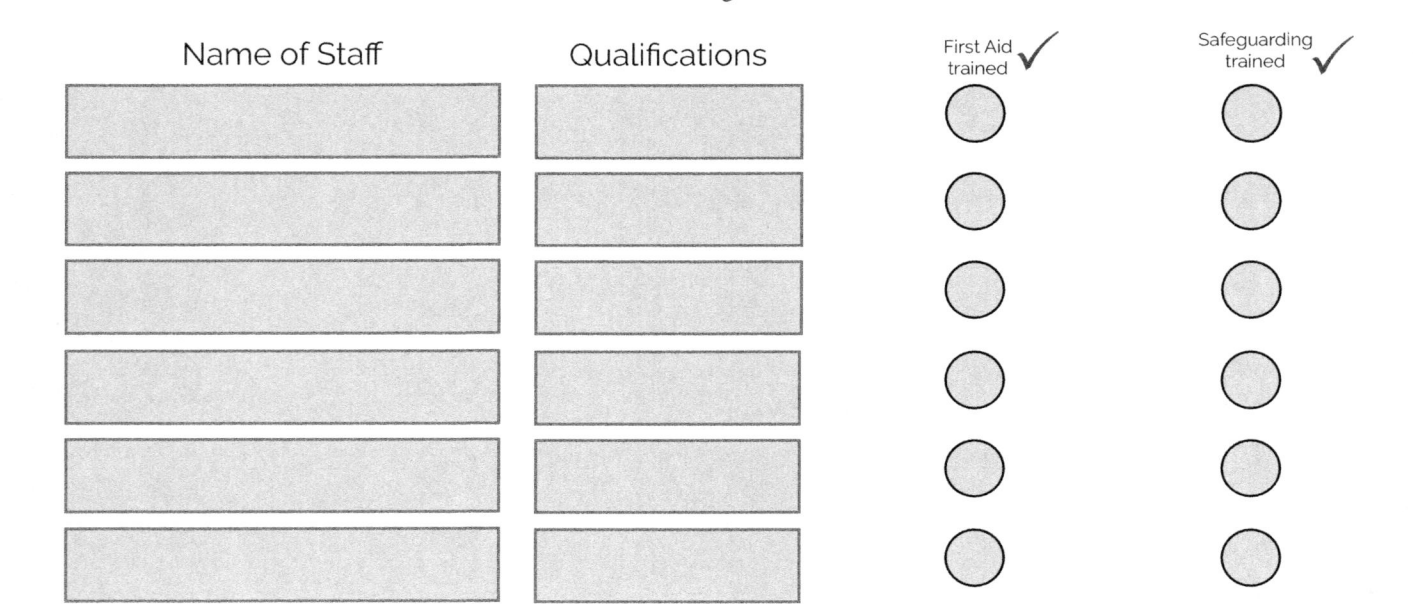

Staffing

Name of Staff	Qualifications	First Aid trained ✓	Safeguarding trained ✓
		○	○
		○	○
		○	○
		○	○
		○	○
		○	○

Date

Name of room

Age of room

Ratio in room

:

Number of children in today

Number of children with EAL

Number of children with SEN

Number of 2 year old funded children

Number of 3 year old funded children

Staffing

Name of Staff	Qualifications	First Aid trained ✓	Safeguarding trained ✓
		○	○
		○	○
		○	○
		○	○
		○	○
		○	○

Date

Name of room

Age of room

Ratio in room

:

Number of children in today

Number of children with EAL

Number of children with SEN

Number of 2 year old funded children

Number of 3 year old funded children

Staffing

Name of Staff	Qualifications	First Aid trained ✓	Safeguarding trained ✓
		◯	◯
		◯	◯
		◯	◯
		◯	◯
		◯	◯
		◯	◯

Jigsaw
EARLY YEARS CONSULTANCY

Jigsaw
EARLY YEARS CONSULTANCY

Date

Name of room	Age of room	Ratio in room
		:

Number of children in today	Number of children with EAL	Number of children with SEN	Number of 2 year old funded children	Number of 3 year old funded children

Staffing

Name of Staff	Qualifications	First Aid trained ✓	Safeguarding trained ✓
		○	○
		○	○
		○	○
		○	○
		○	○
		○	○

Jigsaw
EARLY YEARS CONSULTANCY

Date

Name of room

Age of room

Ratio in room

:

Number of children in today

Number of children with EAL

Number of children with SEN

Number of 2 year old funded children

Number of 3 year old funded children

Staffing

Name of Staff	Qualifications	First Aid trained ✓	Safeguarding trained ✓
		○	○
		○	○
		○	○
		○	○
		○	○
		○	○

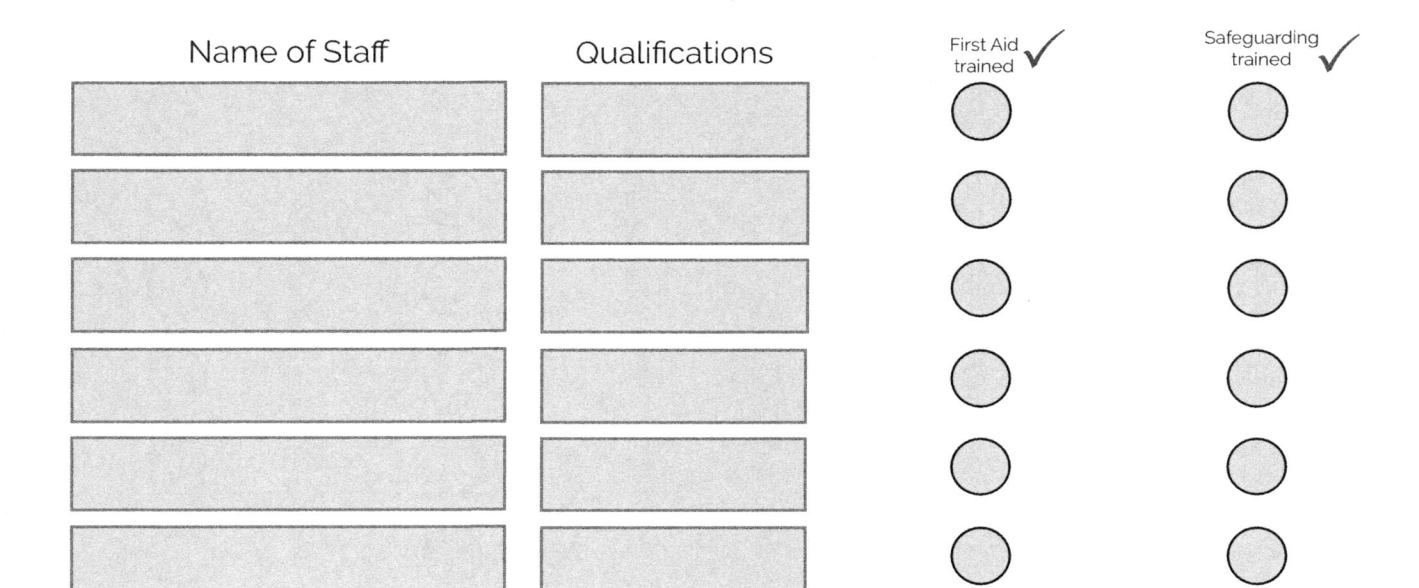

Jigsaw
EARLY YEARS CONSULTANCY

Date

Name of room	Age of room	Ratio in room
		:

Number of children in today	Number of children with EAL	Number of children with SEN	Number of 2 year old funded children	Number of 3 year old funded children

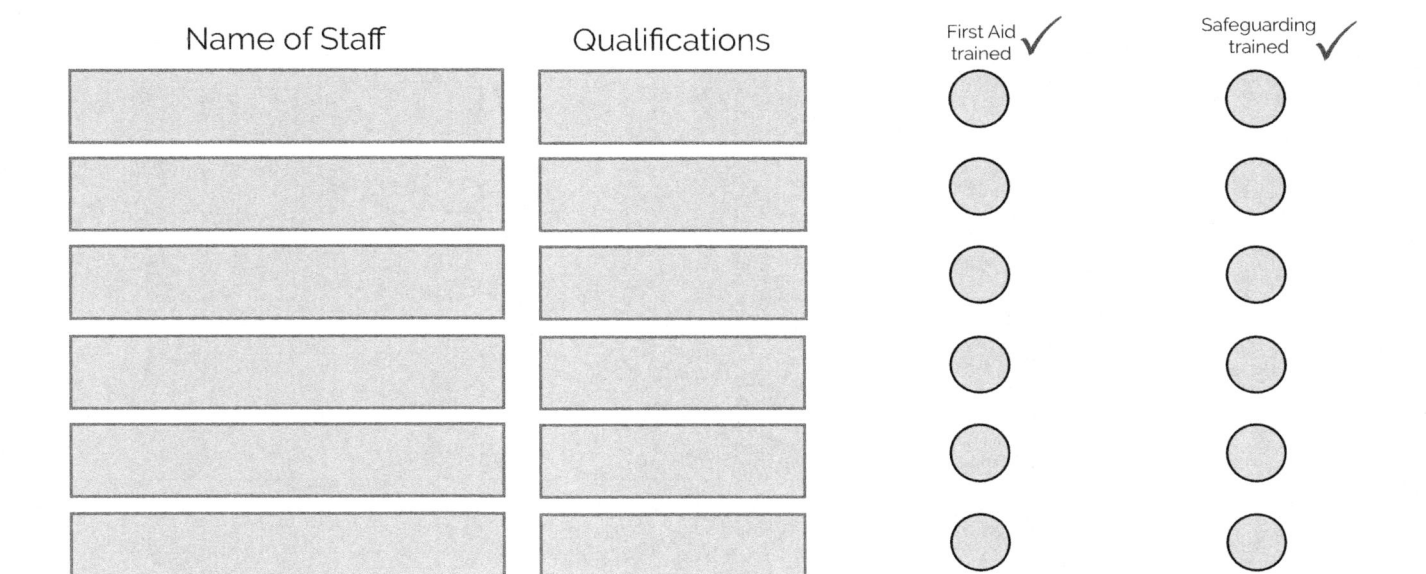

Staffing

Name of Staff	Qualifications	First Aid trained ✓	Safeguarding trained ✓
		○	○
		○	○
		○	○
		○	○
		○	○
		○	○

Jigsaw
EARLY YEARS CONSULTANCY

Date

Name of room

Age of room

Ratio in room

:

Number of children in today

Number of children with EAL

Number of children with SEN

Number of 2 year old funded children

Number of 3 year old funded children

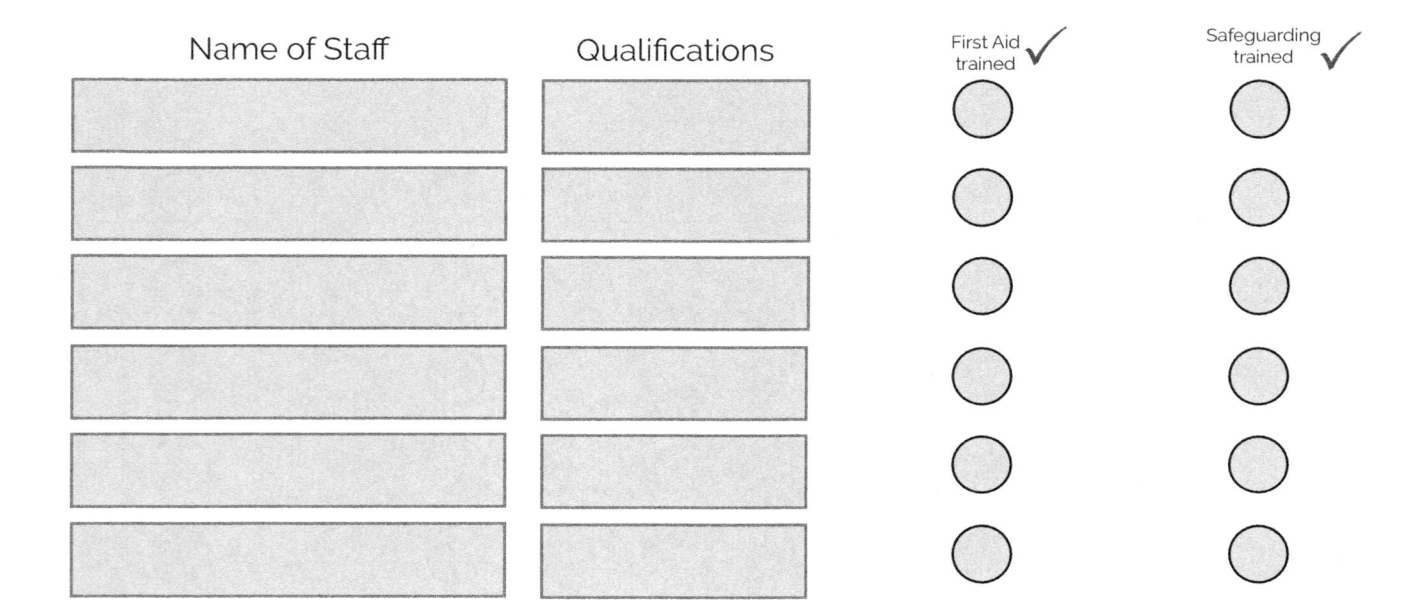

Staffing

Name of Staff	Qualifications	First Aid trained ✓	Safeguarding trained ✓
		○	○
		○	○
		○	○
		○	○
		○	○
		○	○

Date

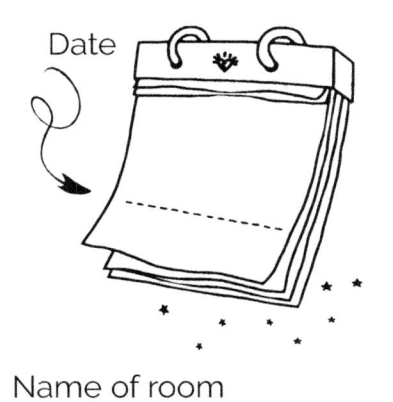

Name of room	Age of room	Ratio in room
		:

Number of children in today	Number of children with EAL	Number of children with SEN	Number of 2 year old funded children	Number of 3 year old funded children

Staffing

Name of Staff	Qualifications	First Aid trained ✓	Safeguarding trained ✓
		○	○
		○	○
		○	○
		○	○
		○	○
		○	○

Date

Name of room

Age of room

Ratio in room

Number of children in today	Number of children with EAL	Number of children with SEN	Number of 2 year old funded children	Number of 3 year old funded children

Staffing

Name of Staff	Qualifications	First Aid trained ✓	Safeguarding trained ✓

Jigsaw
EARLY YEARS CONSULTANCY

Date

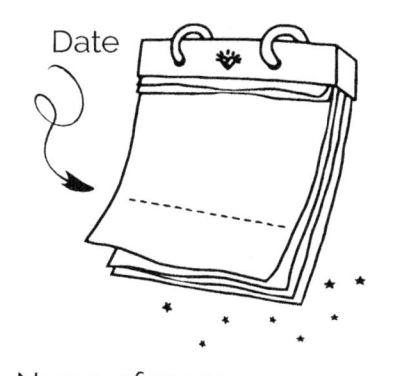

Name of room	Age of room	Ratio in room
		:

Number of children in today	Number of children with EAL	Number of children with SEN	Number of 2 year old funded children	Number of 3 year old funded children

Staffing

Name of Staff	Qualifications	First Aid trained ✓	Safeguarding trained ✓
		○	○
		○	○
		○	○
		○	○
		○	○
		○	○

Date

Name of room	Age of room	Ratio in room
		:

Number of children in today	Number of children with EAL	Number of children with SEN	Number of 2 year old funded children	Number of 3 year old funded children

Staffing

Name of Staff	Qualifications	First Aid trained ✓	Safeguarding trained ✓
		○	○
		○	○
		○	○
		○	○
		○	○
		○	○

Date

Jigsaw
EARLY YEARS CONSULTANCY

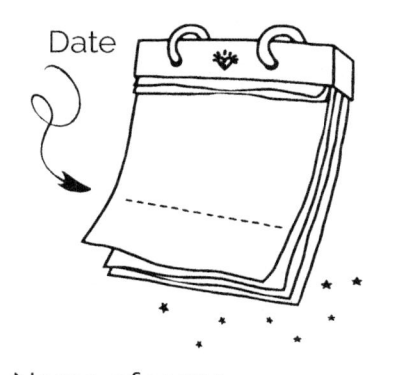

Name of room	Age of room	Ratio in room
		:

Number of children in today	Number of children with EAL	Number of children with SEN	Number of 2 year old funded children	Number of 3 year old funded children

Staffing

Name of Staff	Qualifications	First Aid trained ✓	Safeguarding trained ✓
		◯	◯
		◯	◯
		◯	◯
		◯	◯
		◯	◯
		◯	◯

Jigsaw
EARLY YEARS CONSULTANCY

Date

Name of room	Age of room	Ratio in room
		:

Number of children in today	Number of children with EAL	Number of children with SEN	Number of 2 year old funded children	Number of 3 year old funded children

Staffing

Name of Staff	Qualifications	First Aid trained ✓	Safeguarding trained ✓
		○	○
		○	○
		○	○
		○	○
		○	○
		○	○

Date

Jigsaw
EARLY YEARS CONSULTANCY

Name of room	Age of room	Ratio in room
		:

Number of children in today	Number of children with EAL	Number of children with SEN	Number of 2 year old funded children	Number of 3 year old funded children

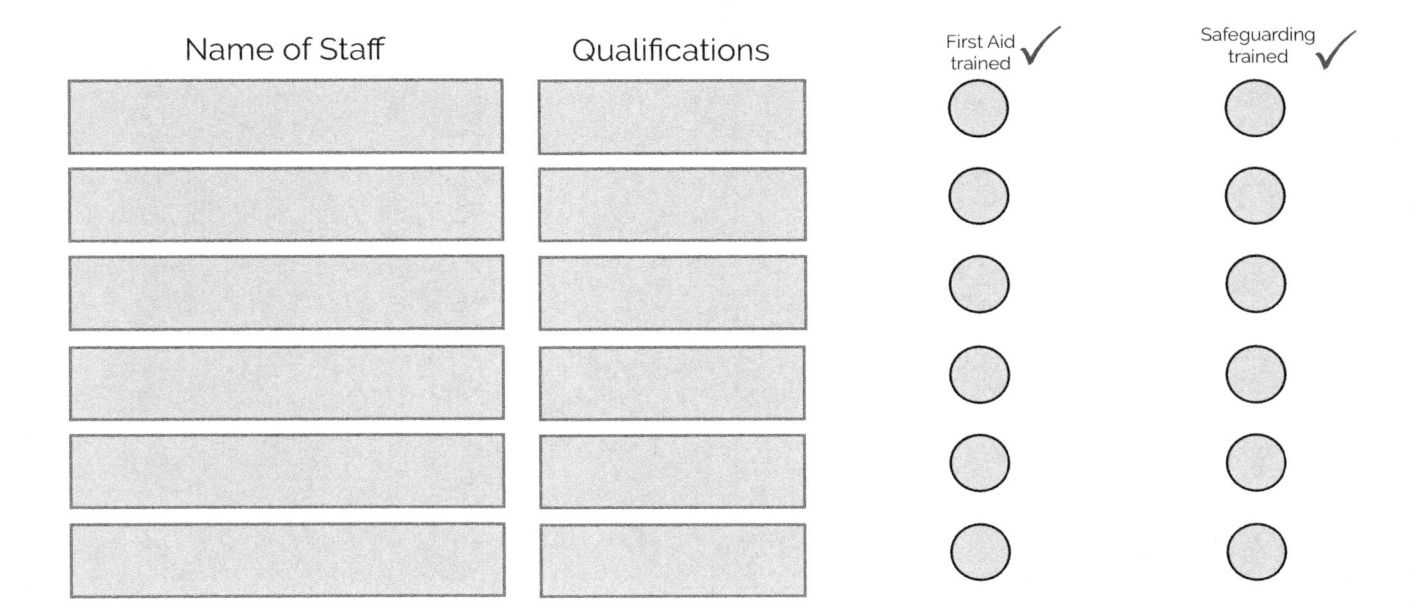

Staffing

Name of Staff	Qualifications	First Aid trained ✓	Safeguarding trained ✓
		○	○
		○	○
		○	○
		○	○
		○	○
		○	○

Date

Jigsaw
EARLY YEARS CONSULTANCY

Name of room	Age of room	Ratio in room
		:

Number of children in today	Number of children with EAL	Number of children with SEN	Number of 2 year old funded children	Number of 3 year old funded children

Staffing

Name of Staff	Qualifications	First Aid trained ✓	Safeguarding trained ✓
		○	○
		○	○
		○	○
		○	○
		○	○
		○	○

Jigsaw
EARLY YEARS CONSULTANCY

Date

Name of room

Age of room

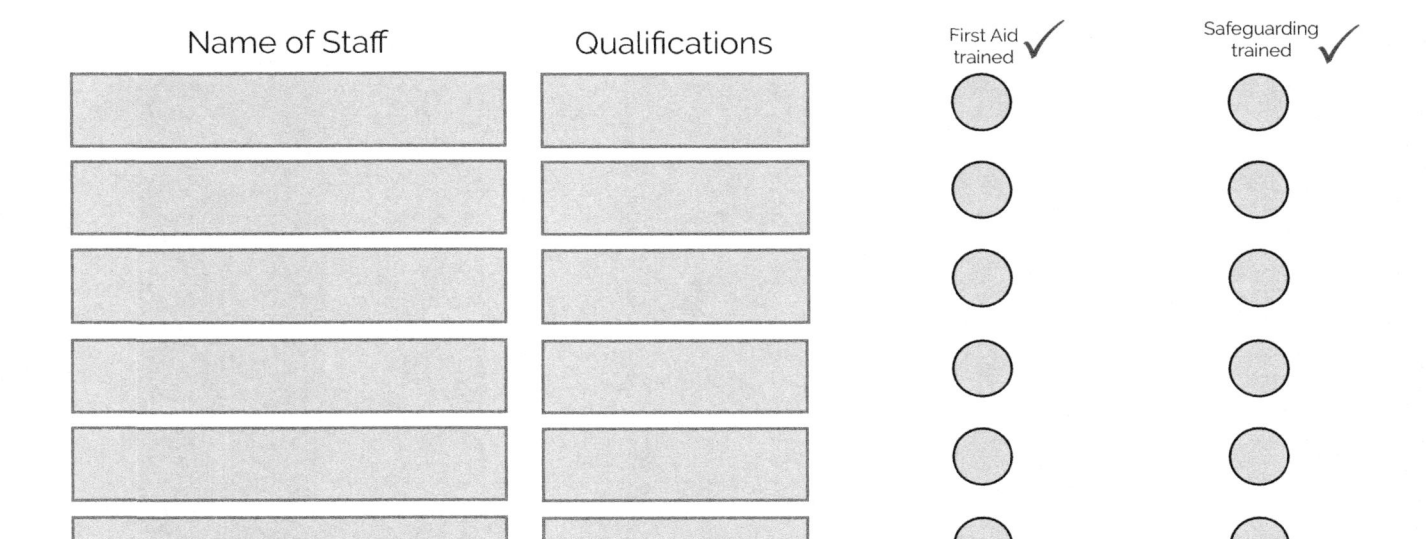

Ratio in room

:

Number of children in today

Number of children with EAL

Number of children with SEN

Number of 2 year old funded children

Number of 3 year old funded children

Staffing

Name of Staff	Qualifications	First Aid trained ✓	Safeguarding trained ✓
		○	○
		○	○
		○	○
		○	○
		○	○
		○	○

Jigsaw
EARLY YEARS CONSULTANCY

Date

Name of room	Age of room	Ratio in room
		:

Number of children in today	Number of children with EAL	Number of children with SEN	Number of 2 year old funded children	Number of 3 year old funded children

Staffing

Name of Staff	Qualifications	First Aid trained ✓	Safeguarding trained ✓
		○	○
		○	○
		○	○
		○	○
		○	○
		○	○

Jigsaw
EARLY YEARS CONSULTANCY

Date

Name of room	Age of room	Ratio in room
		:

Number of children in today	Number of children with EAL	Number of children with SEN	Number of 2 year old funded children	Number of 3 year old funded children

Staffing

Name of Staff	Qualifications	First Aid trained ✓	Safeguarding trained ✓
		○	○
		○	○
		○	○
		○	○
		○	○
		○	○

Date

Name of room

Age of room

Ratio in room

:

Number of children in today

Number of children with EAL

Number of children with SEN

Number of 2 year old funded children

Number of 3 year old funded children

Staffing

Name of Staff	Qualifications	First Aid trained ✓	Safeguarding trained ✓

Jigsaw
EARLY YEARS CONSULTANCY

Date

Name of room	Age of room	Ratio in room
		:

Number of children in today	Number of children with EAL	Number of children with SEN	Number of 2 year old funded children	Number of 3 year old funded children

Staffing

Name of Staff	Qualifications	First Aid trained ✓	Safeguarding trained ✓
		○	○
		○	○
		○	○
		○	○
		○	○
		○	○

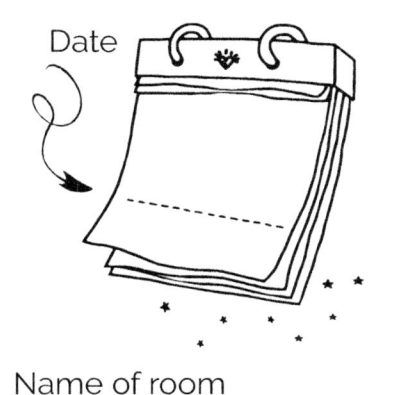

Jigsaw
EARLY YEARS CONSULTANCY

Date

Name of room

Age of room

Ratio in room

Number of children in today	Number of children with EAL	Number of children with SEN	Number of 2 year old funded children	Number of 3 year old funded children

Staffing

Name of Staff	Qualifications	First Aid trained ✓	Safeguarding trained ✓

Jigsaw
EARLY YEARS CONSULTANCY

Date

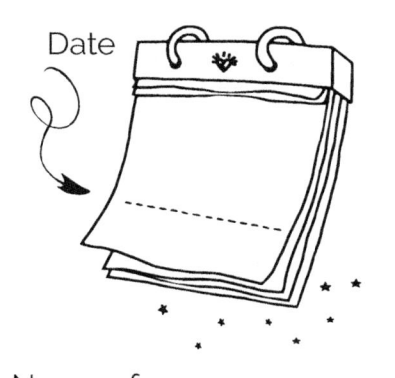

Name of room	Age of room	Ratio in room
		:

Number of children in today	Number of children with EAL	Number of children with SEN	Number of 2 year old funded children	Number of 3 year old funded children

Staffing

Name of Staff	Qualifications	First Aid trained ✓	Safeguarding trained ✓
		○	○
		○	○
		○	○
		○	○
		○	○
		○	○

Jigsaw
EARLY YEARS CONSULTANCY

Date

Name of room	Age of room	Ratio in room
		:

Number of children in today	Number of children with EAL	Number of children with SEN	Number of 2 year old funded children	Number of 3 year old funded children

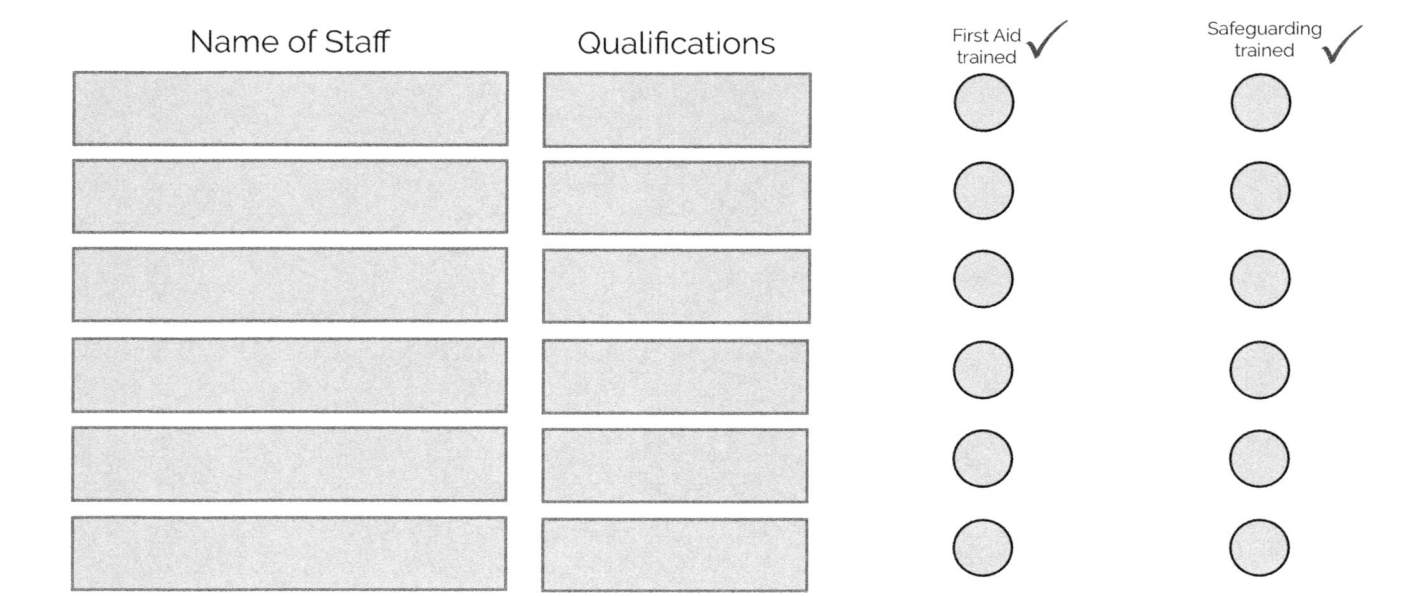

Staffing

Name of Staff	Qualifications	First Aid trained ✓	Safeguarding trained ✓
		○	○
		○	○
		○	○
		○	○
		○	○
		○	○

Jigsaw
EARLY YEARS CONSULTANCY

Date

Name of room	Age of room	Ratio in room
		:

Number of children in today	Number of children with EAL	Number of children with SEN	Number of 2 year old funded children	Number of 3 year old funded children

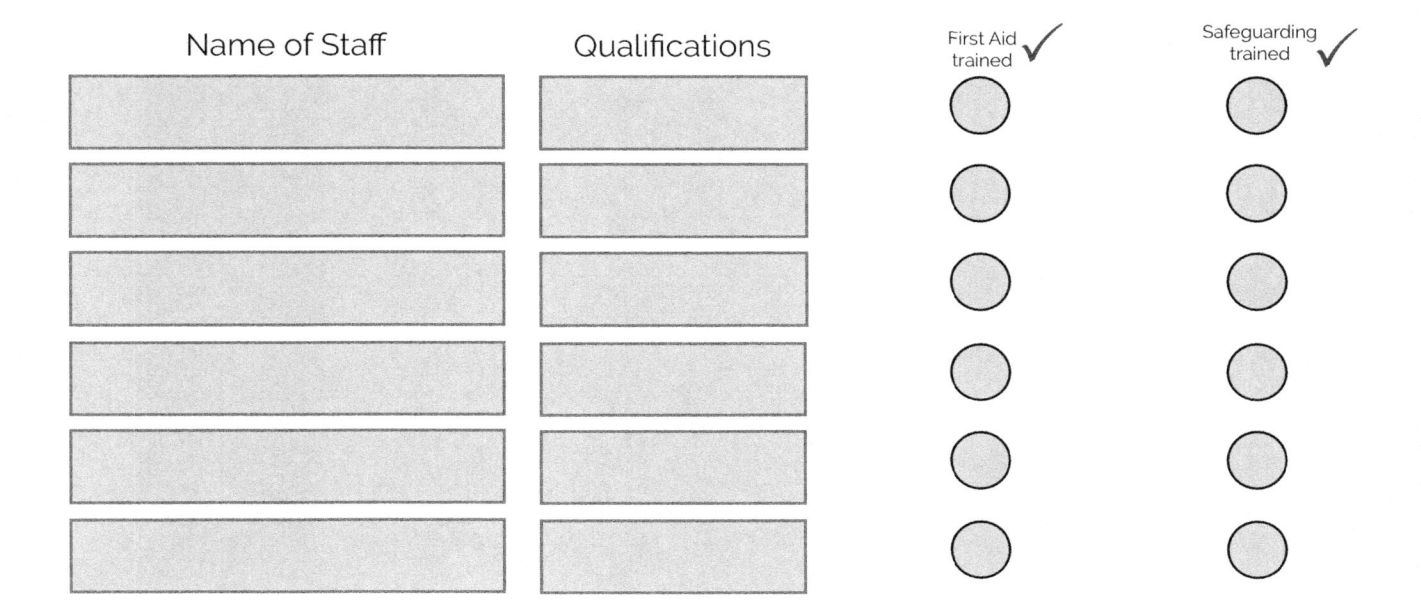

Staffing

Name of Staff	Qualifications	First Aid trained ✓	Safeguarding trained ✓
		○	○
		○	○
		○	○
		○	○
		○	○
		○	○

Jigsaw
EARLY YEARS CONSULTANCY

Date

Name of room

Age of room

Ratio in room

| : |

Number of children in today

Number of children with EAL

Number of children with SEN

Number of 2 year old funded children

Number of 3 year old funded children

Staffing

Name of Staff	Qualifications	First Aid trained ✓	Safeguarding trained ✓
		○	○
		○	○
		○	○
		○	○
		○	○
		○	○

Jigsaw
EARLY YEARS CONSULTANCY

Date

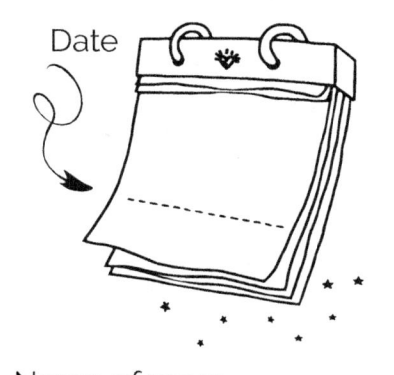

Name of room	Age of room	Ratio in room
		:

Number of children in today	Number of children with EAL	Number of children with SEN	Number of 2 year old funded children	Number of 3 year old funded children

Staffing

Name of Staff	Qualifications	First Aid trained ✓	Safeguarding trained ✓
		○	○
		○	○
		○	○
		○	○
		○	○
		○	○

Date

Name of room

Age of room

Ratio in room

:

Number of children in today

Number of children with EAL

Number of children with SEN

Number of 2 year old funded children

Number of 3 year old funded children

Staffing

Name of Staff	Qualifications	First Aid trained ✓	Safeguarding trained ✓
		○	○
		○	○
		○	○
		○	○
		○	○
		○	○

Jigsaw
EARLY YEARS CONSULTANCY

Date

Name of room	Age of room	Ratio in room
		:

Number of children in today	Number of children with EAL	Number of children with SEN	Number of 2 year old funded children	Number of 3 year old funded children

Staffing

Name of Staff	Qualifications	First Aid trained ✓	Safeguarding trained ✓
		○	○
		○	○
		○	○
		○	○
		○	○
		○	○

Date

Name of room

Age of room

Ratio in room

:

Number of children in today	Number of children with EAL	Number of children with SEN	Number of 2 year old funded children	Number of 3 year old funded children

Staffing

Name of Staff	Qualifications	First Aid trained ✓	Safeguarding trained ✓

Date

Name of room

Age of room

Ratio in room

Number of children in today	Number of children with EAL	Number of children with SEN	Number of 2 year old funded children	Number of 3 year old funded children

Staffing

Name of Staff	Qualifications	First Aid trained ✓	Safeguarding trained ✓

Jigsaw
EARLY YEARS CONSULTANCY

Date

Name of room

Age of room

Ratio in room

:

Number of children in today

Number of children with EAL

Number of children with SEN

Number of 2 year old funded children

Number of 3 year old funded children

Staffing

Name of Staff	Qualifications	First Aid trained ✓	Safeguarding trained ✓
		◯	◯
		◯	◯
		◯	◯
		◯	◯
		◯	◯
		◯	◯

Jigsaw
EARLY YEARS CONSULTANCY

Date

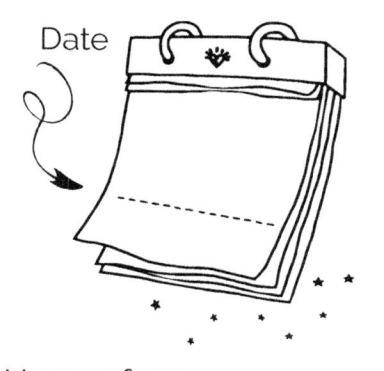

Name of room	Age of room	Ratio in room
		:

Number of children in today	Number of children with EAL	Number of children with SEN	Number of 2 year old funded children	Number of 3 year old funded children

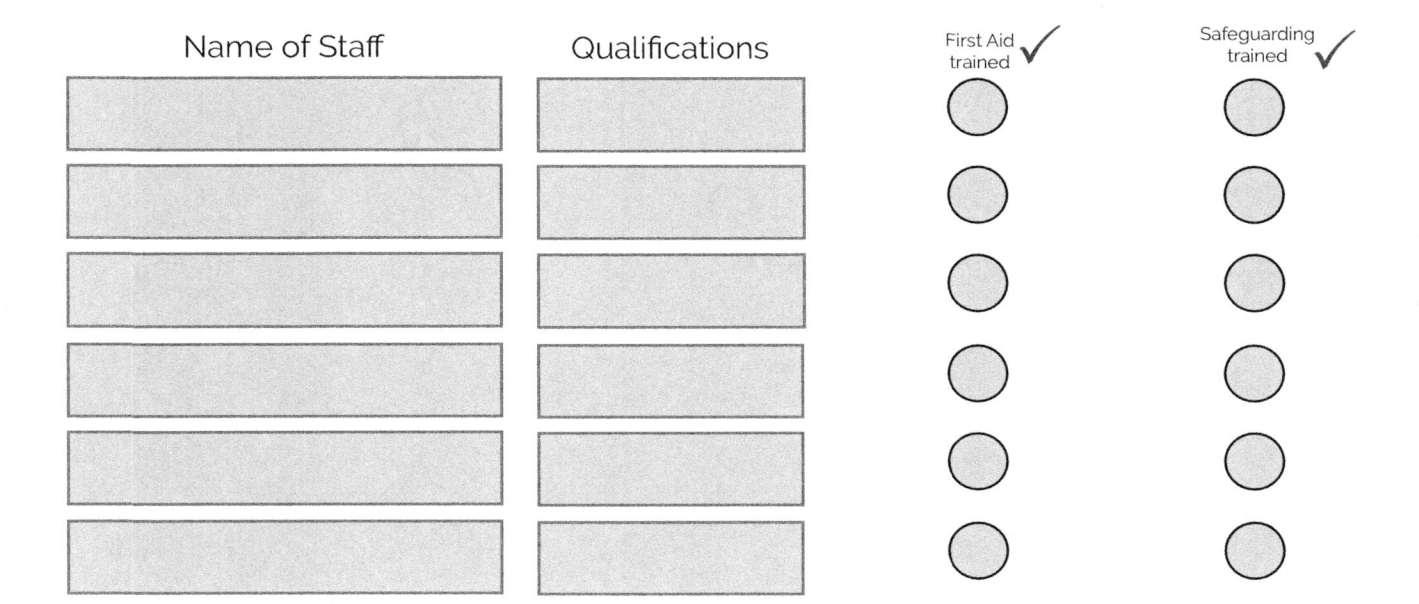

Staffing

Name of Staff	Qualifications	First Aid trained ✓	Safeguarding trained ✓
		○	○
		○	○
		○	○
		○	○
		○	○
		○	○

Date

Name of room

Age of room

Ratio in room

:

Number of children in today

Number of children with EAL

Number of children with SEN

Number of 2 year old funded children

Number of 3 year old funded children

Staffing

Name of Staff	Qualifications	First Aid trained ✓	Safeguarding trained ✓
		○	○
		○	○
		○	○
		○	○
		○	○
		○	○

Jigsaw Early Years Consultancy

Date

Name of room

Age of room

Ratio in room

:

Number of children in today	Number of children with EAL	Number of children with SEN	Number of 2 year old funded children	Number of 3 year old funded children

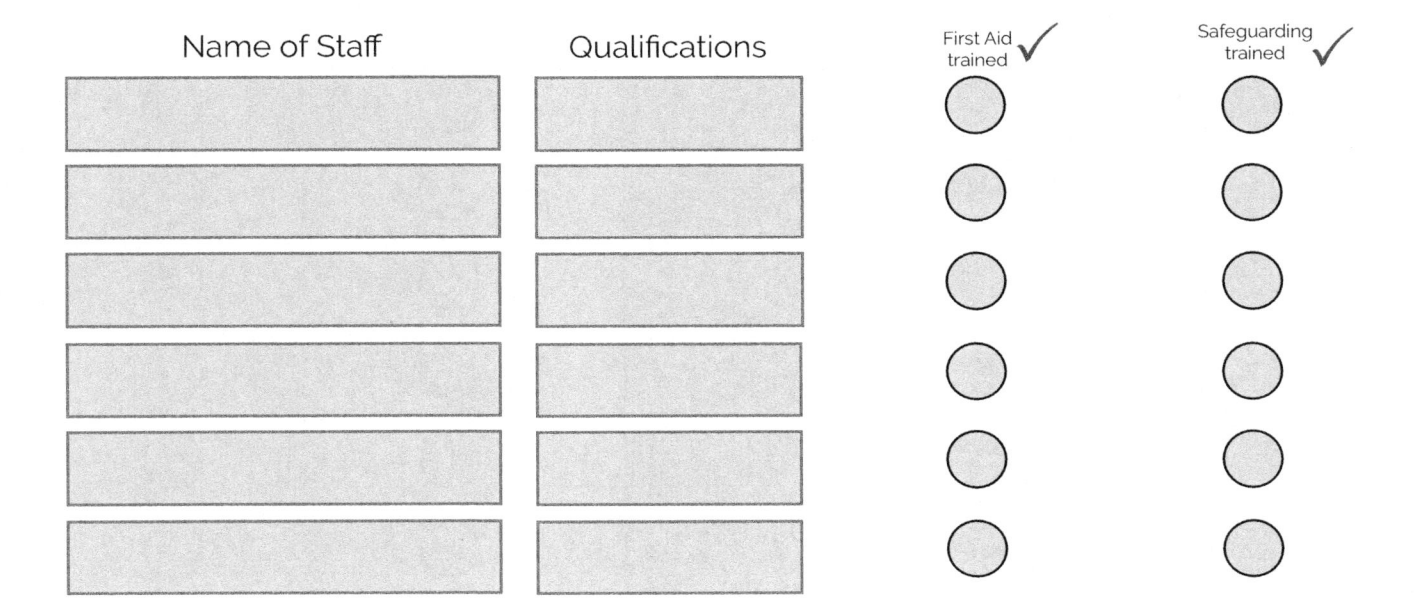

Staffing

Name of Staff	Qualifications	First Aid trained ✓	Safeguarding trained ✓
		○	○
		○	○
		○	○
		○	○
		○	○
		○	○

Jigsaw
EARLY YEARS CONSULTANCY

Jigsaw
EARLY YEARS CONSULTANCY

Date

Name of room	Age of room	Ratio in room
		:

Number of children in today	Number of children with EAL	Number of children with SEN	Number of 2 year old funded children	Number of 3 year old funded children

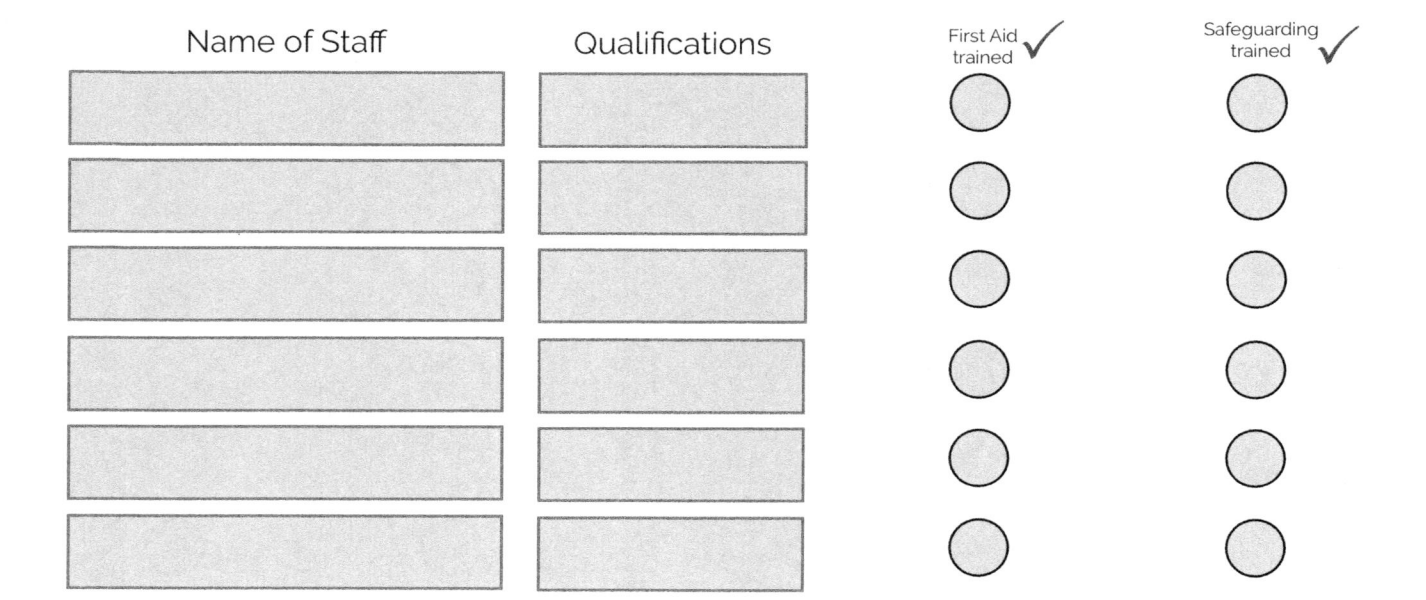

Staffing

Name of Staff	Qualifications	First Aid trained ✓	Safeguarding trained ✓
		◯	◯
		◯	◯
		◯	◯
		◯	◯
		◯	◯
		◯	◯

Date

Name of room	Age of room	Ratio in room
		:

Number of children in today	Number of children with EAL	Number of children with SEN	Number of 2 year old funded children	Number of 3 year old funded children

Staffing

Name of Staff	Qualifications	First Aid trained ✓	Safeguarding trained ✓
		○	○
		○	○
		○	○
		○	○
		○	○
		○	○

Jigsaw
EARLY YEARS CONSULTANCY

Date

Name of room

Age of room

Ratio in room

Number of children in today

Number of children with EAL

Number of children with SEN

Number of 2 year old funded children

Number of 3 year old funded children

Staffing

Name of Staff	Qualifications	First Aid trained ✓	Safeguarding trained ✓
		○	○
		○	○
		○	○
		○	○
		○	○
		○	○

Jigsaw
EARLY YEARS CONSULTANCY

Date

Name of room	Age of room	Ratio in room
		:

Number of children in today	Number of children with EAL	Number of children with SEN	Number of 2 year old funded children	Number of 3 year old funded children

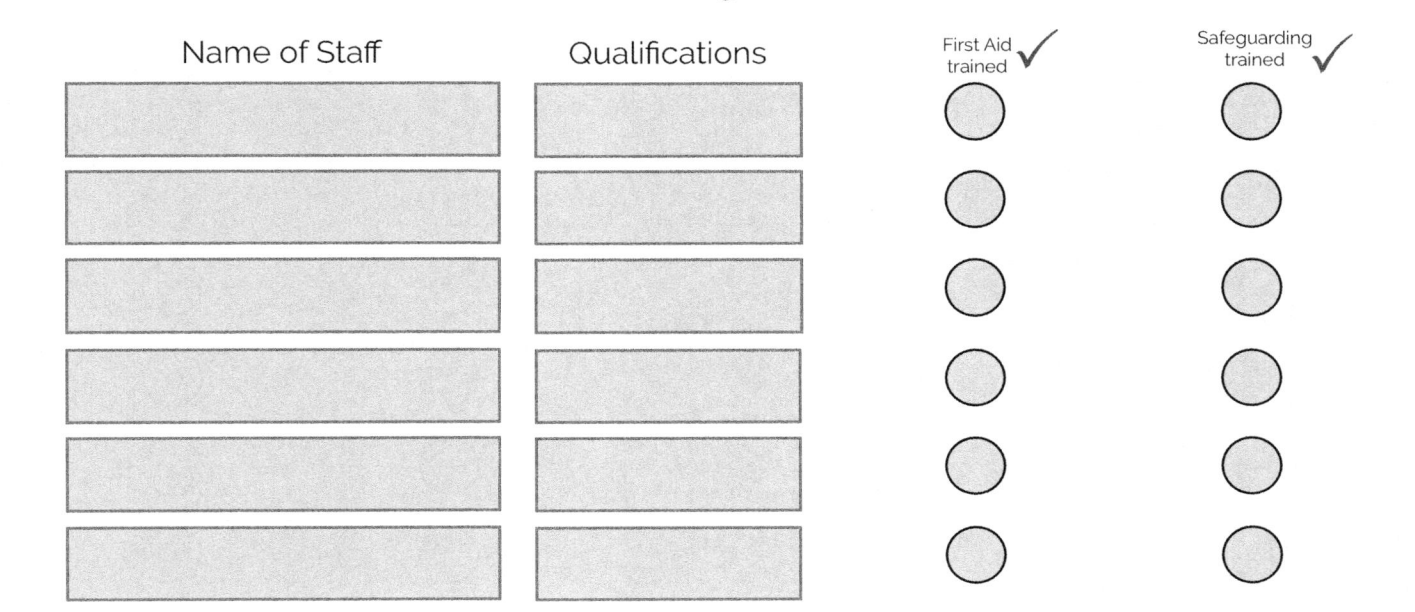

Staffing

Name of Staff	Qualifications	First Aid trained ✓	Safeguarding trained ✓
		◯	◯
		◯	◯
		◯	◯
		◯	◯
		◯	◯
		◯	◯

Date

Name of room

Age of room

Ratio in room

:

Number of children in today	Number of children with EAL	Number of children with SEN	Number of 2 year old funded children	Number of 3 year old funded children

Staffing

Name of Staff	Qualifications	First Aid trained ✓	Safeguarding trained ✓

Date

Name of room

Age of room

Ratio in room

:

Number of children in today	Number of children with EAL	Number of children with SEN	Number of 2 year old funded children	Number of 3 year old funded children

Staffing

Name of Staff	Qualifications	First Aid trained ✓	Safeguarding trained ✓

Jigsaw
EARLY YEARS CONSULTANCY

Date

Name of room	Age of room	Ratio in room
		:

Number of children in today	Number of children with EAL	Number of children with SEN	Number of 2 year old funded children	Number of 3 year old funded children

Staffing

Name of Staff	Qualifications	First Aid trained ✓	Safeguarding trained ✓
		○	○
		○	○
		○	○
		○	○
		○	○
		○	○

Jigsaw
EARLY YEARS CONSULTANCY

Date

Name of room

Age of room

Ratio in room

:

Number of children in today

Number of children with EAL

Number of children with SEN

Number of 2 year old funded children

Number of 3 year old funded children

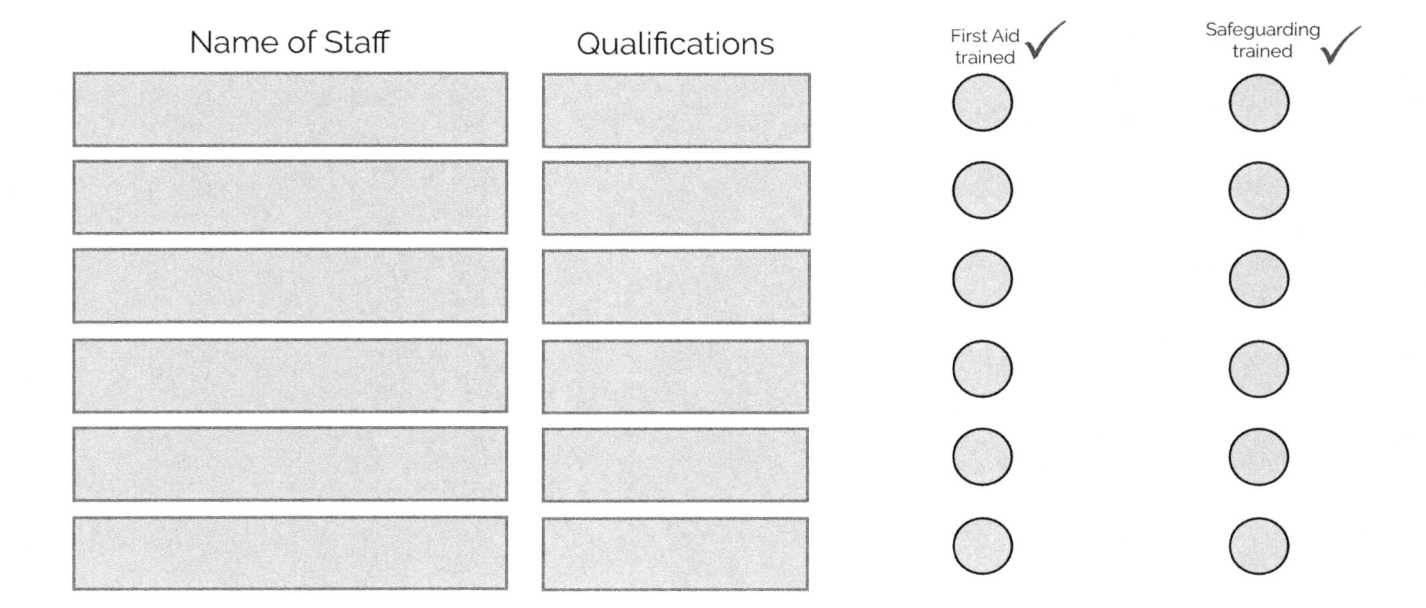

Staffing

Name of Staff	Qualifications	First Aid trained ✓	Safeguarding trained ✓
		○	○
		○	○
		○	○
		○	○
		○	○
		○	○

Jigsaw
EARLY YEARS CONSULTANCY

Date

Name of room

Age of room

Ratio in room

Number of children in today	Number of children with EAL	Number of children with SEN	Number of 2 year old funded children	Number of 3 year old funded children

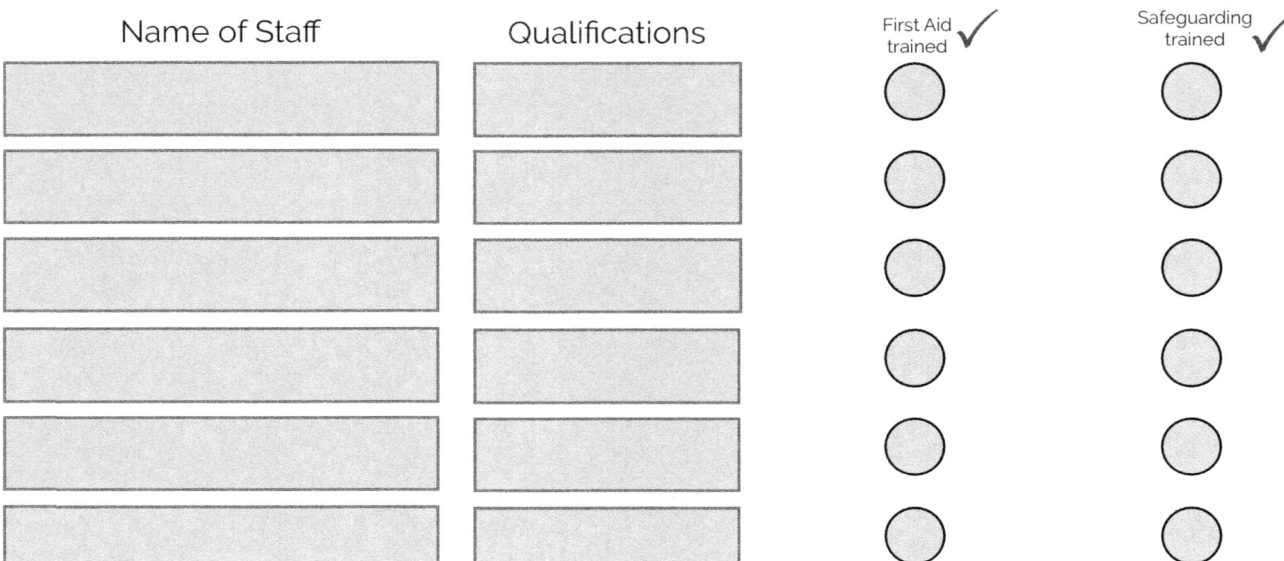

Staffing

Name of Staff	Qualifications	First Aid trained ✓	Safeguarding trained ✓

Date

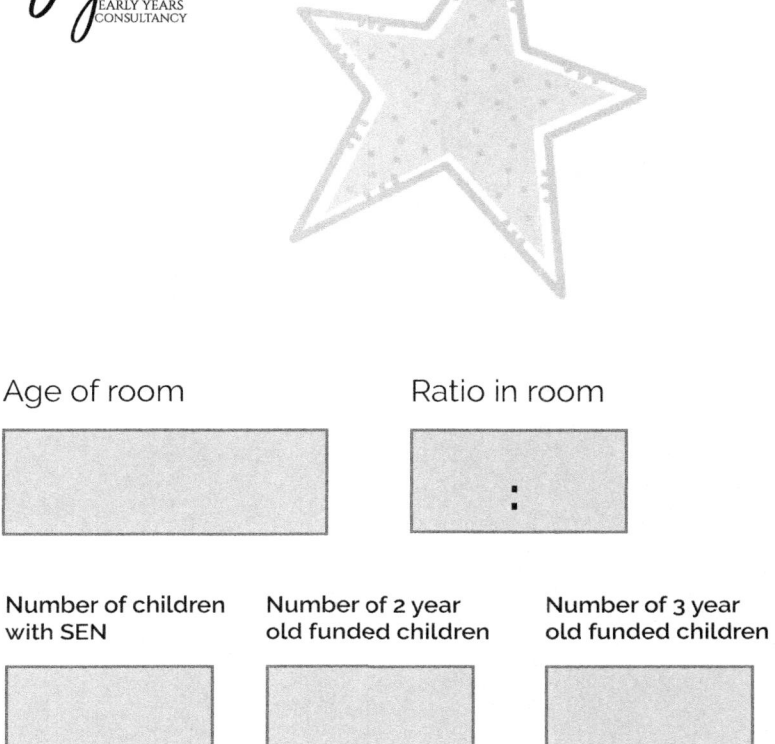

Name of room

Age of room

Ratio in room

:

Number of children in today	Number of children with EAL	Number of children with SEN	Number of 2 year old funded children	Number of 3 year old funded children

Staffing

Name of Staff	Qualifications	First Aid trained ✓	Safeguarding trained ✓
		◯	◯
		◯	◯
		◯	◯
		◯	◯
		◯	◯
		◯	◯

Jigsaw
EARLY YEARS CONSULTANCY

Date

Name of room	Age of room	Ratio in room
		:

Number of children in today	Number of children with EAL	Number of children with SEN	Number of 2 year old funded children	Number of 3 year old funded children

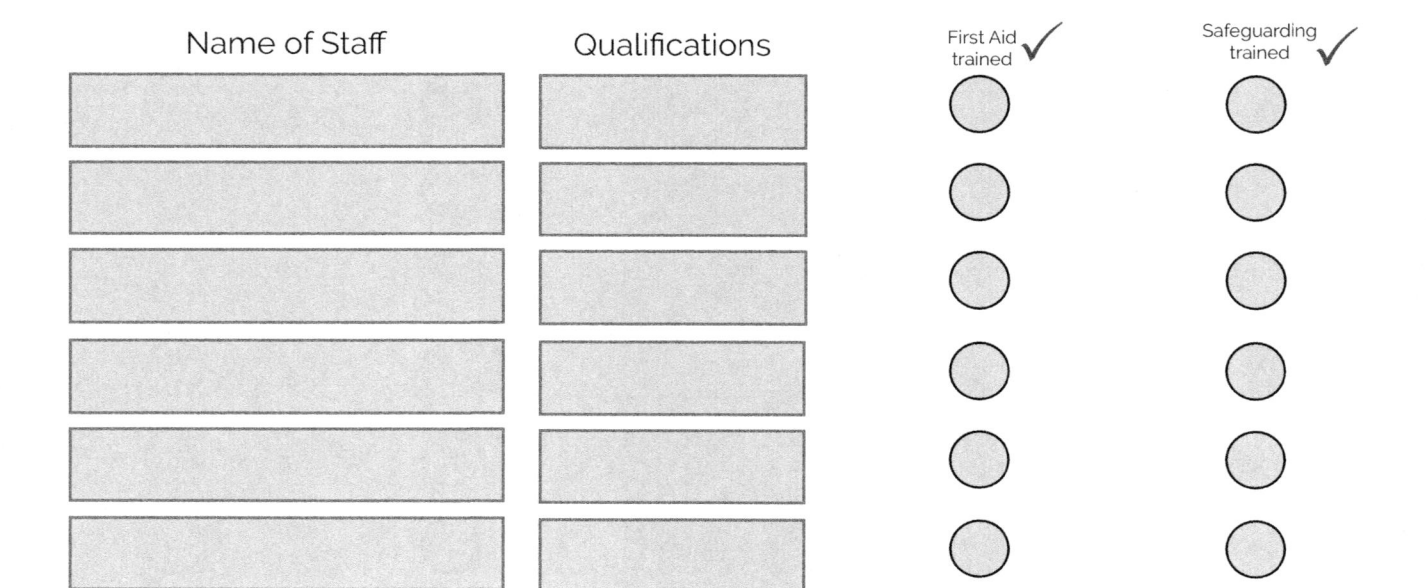

Staffing

Name of Staff	Qualifications	First Aid trained ✓	Safeguarding trained ✓
		○	○
		○	○
		○	○
		○	○
		○	○
		○	○

Date

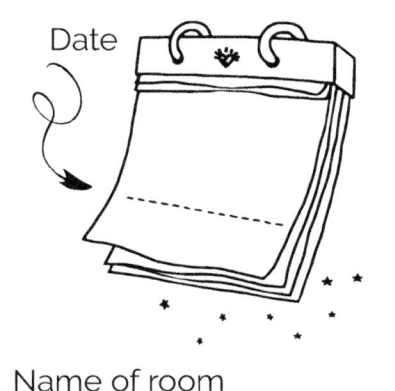

Jigsaw
EARLY YEARS CONSULTANCY

Name of room

Age of room

Ratio in room

Number of children in today	Number of children with EAL	Number of children with SEN	Number of 2 year old funded children	Number of 3 year old funded children

Staffing

Name of Staff	Qualifications	First Aid trained ✓	Safeguarding trained ✓
		○	○
		○	○
		○	○
		○	○
		○	○
		○	○

Date

Jigsaw
EARLY YEARS CONSULTANCY

Name of room	Age of room	Ratio in room
		:

Number of children in today	Number of children with EAL	Number of children with SEN	Number of 2 year old funded children	Number of 3 year old funded children

Staffing

Name of Staff	Qualifications	First Aid trained ✓	Safeguarding trained ✓
		○	○
		○	○
		○	○
		○	○
		○	○
		○	○

Date

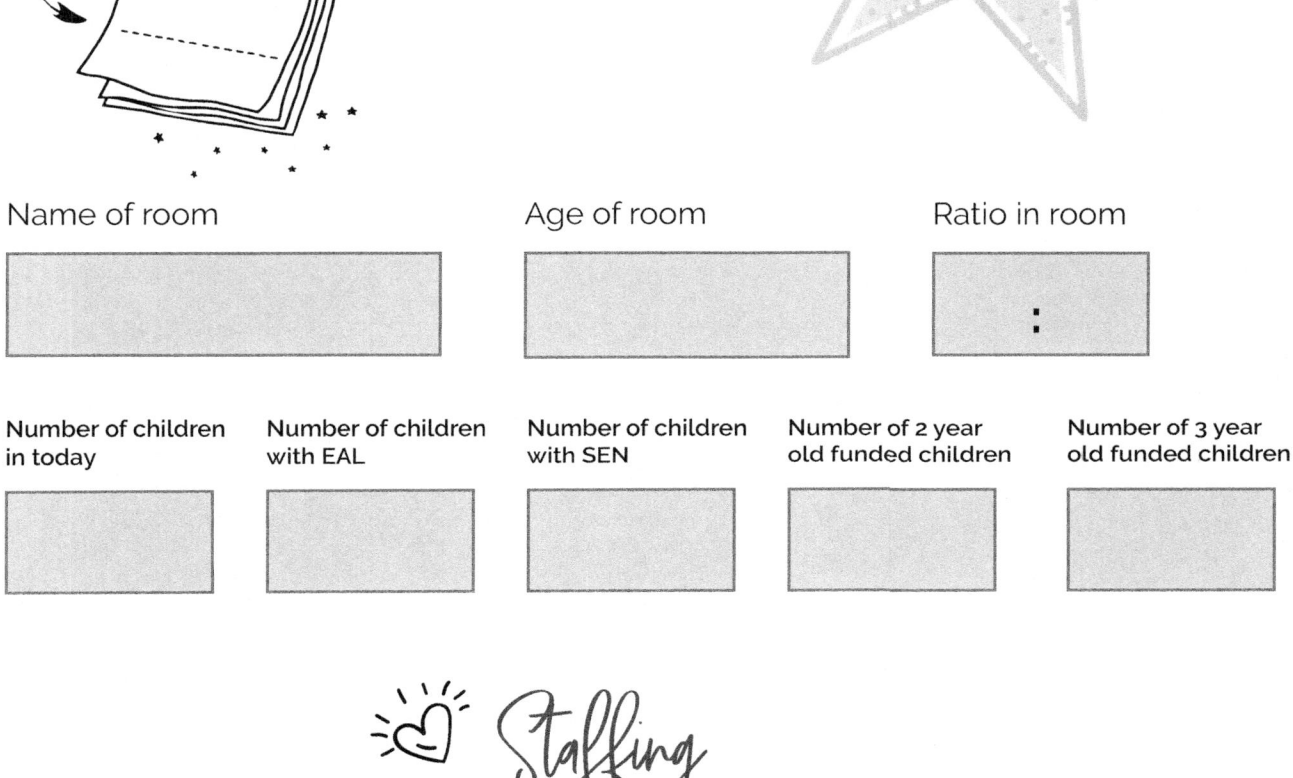

Name of room	Age of room	Ratio in room
		:

Number of children in today	Number of children with EAL	Number of children with SEN	Number of 2 year old funded children	Number of 3 year old funded children

Staffing

Name of Staff	Qualifications	First Aid trained ✓	Safeguarding trained ✓
		○	○
		○	○
		○	○
		○	○
		○	○
		○	○

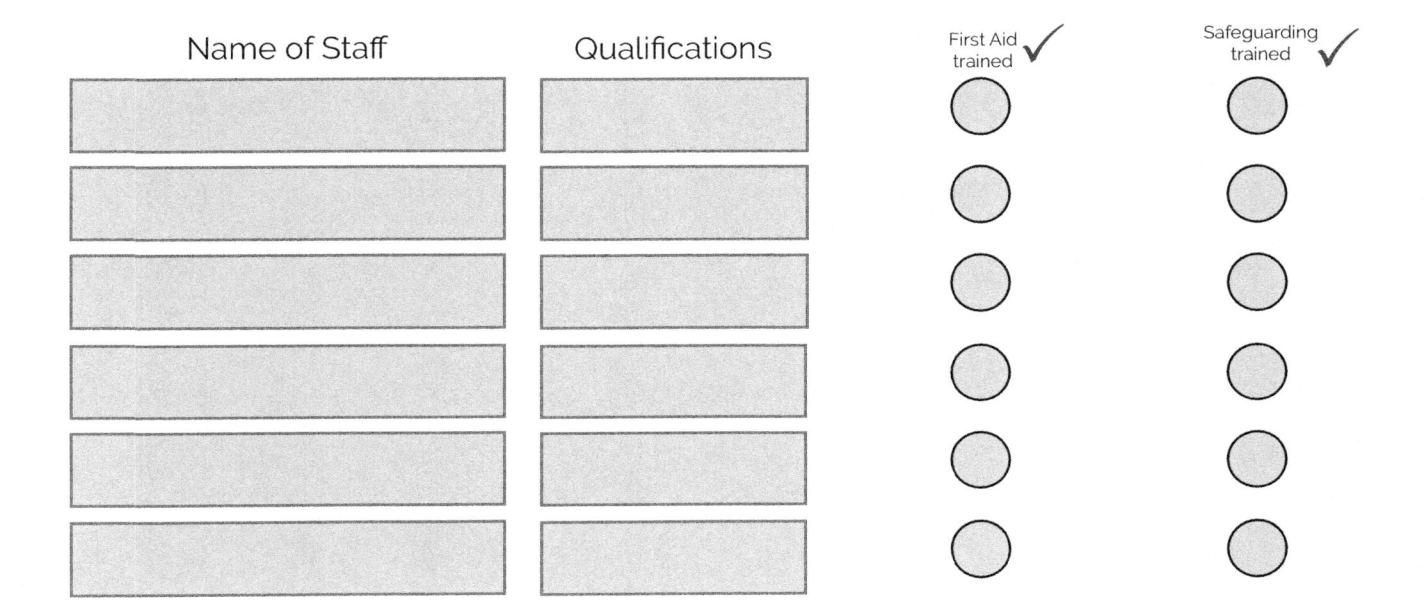

Jigsaw Early Years Consultancy

Date

Name of room	Age of room	Ratio in room
		:

Number of children in today	Number of children with EAL	Number of children with SEN	Number of 2 year old funded children	Number of 3 year old funded children

Staffing

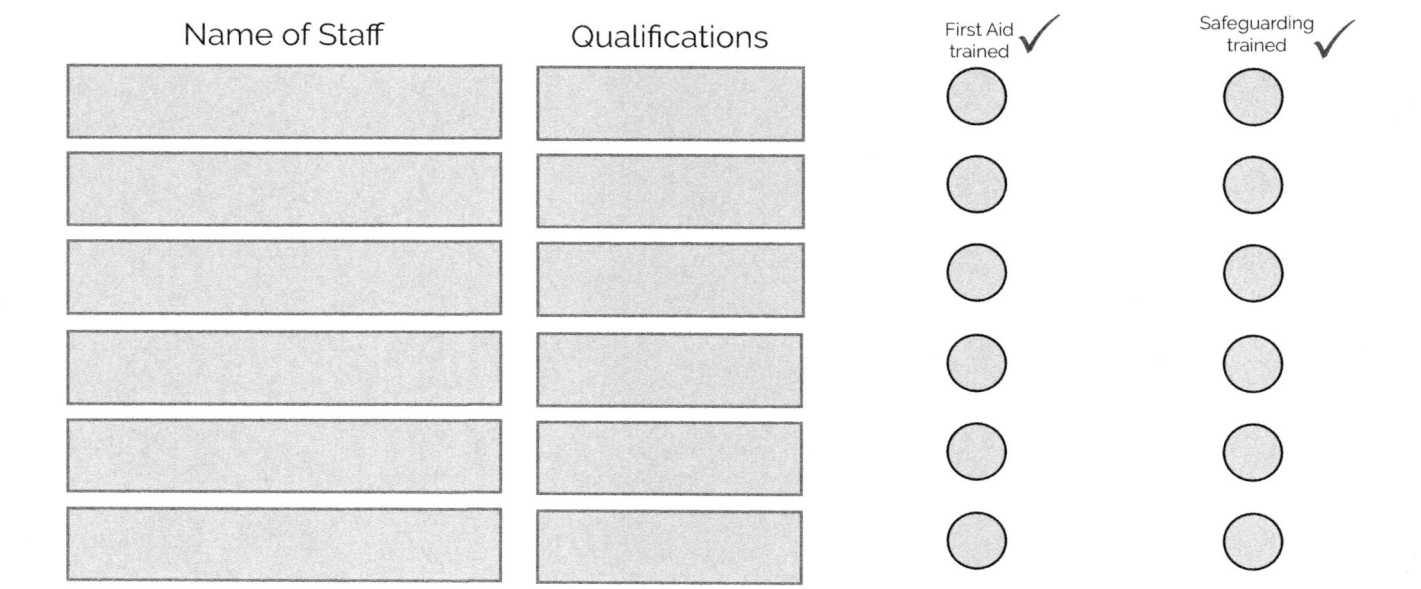

Name of Staff	Qualifications	First Aid trained ✓	Safeguarding trained ✓
		○	○
		○	○
		○	○
		○	○
		○	○
		○	○

Jigsaw
EARLY YEARS CONSULTANCY

Date

Name of room	Age of room	Ratio in room
		:

Number of children in today	Number of children with EAL	Number of children with SEN	Number of 2 year old funded children	Number of 3 year old funded children

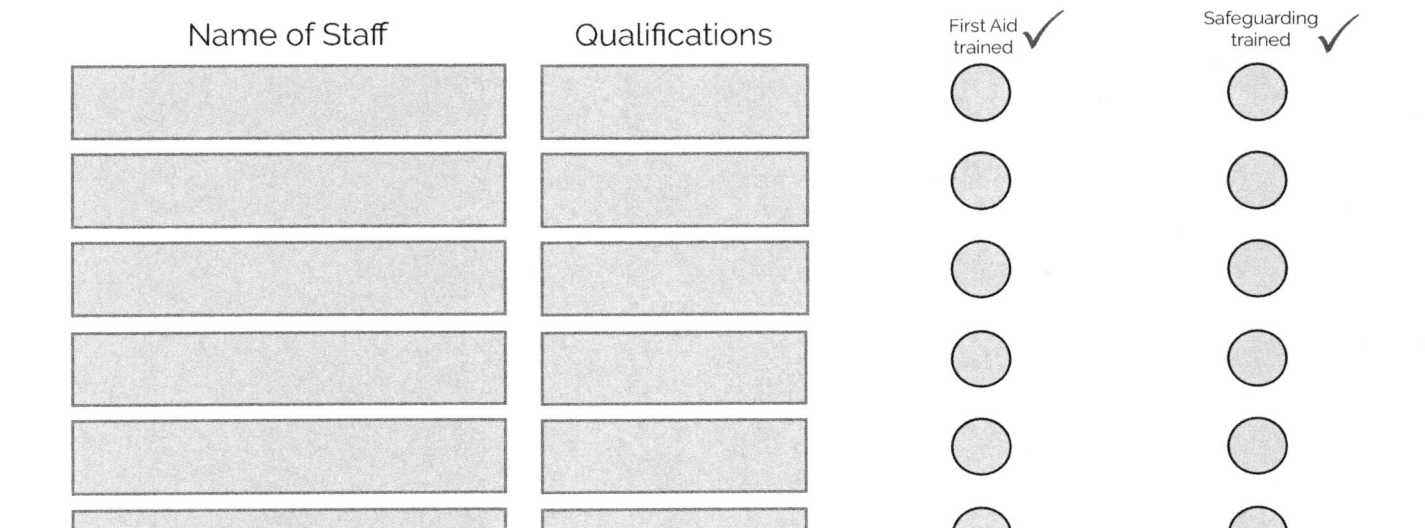

Staffing

Name of Staff	Qualifications	First Aid trained ✓	Safeguarding trained ✓
		○	○
		○	○
		○	○
		○	○
		○	○
		○	○

Jigsaw
EARLY YEARS CONSULTANCY

Date

Name of room	Age of room	Ratio in room
		:

Number of children in today	Number of children with EAL	Number of children with SEN	Number of 2 year old funded children	Number of 3 year old funded children

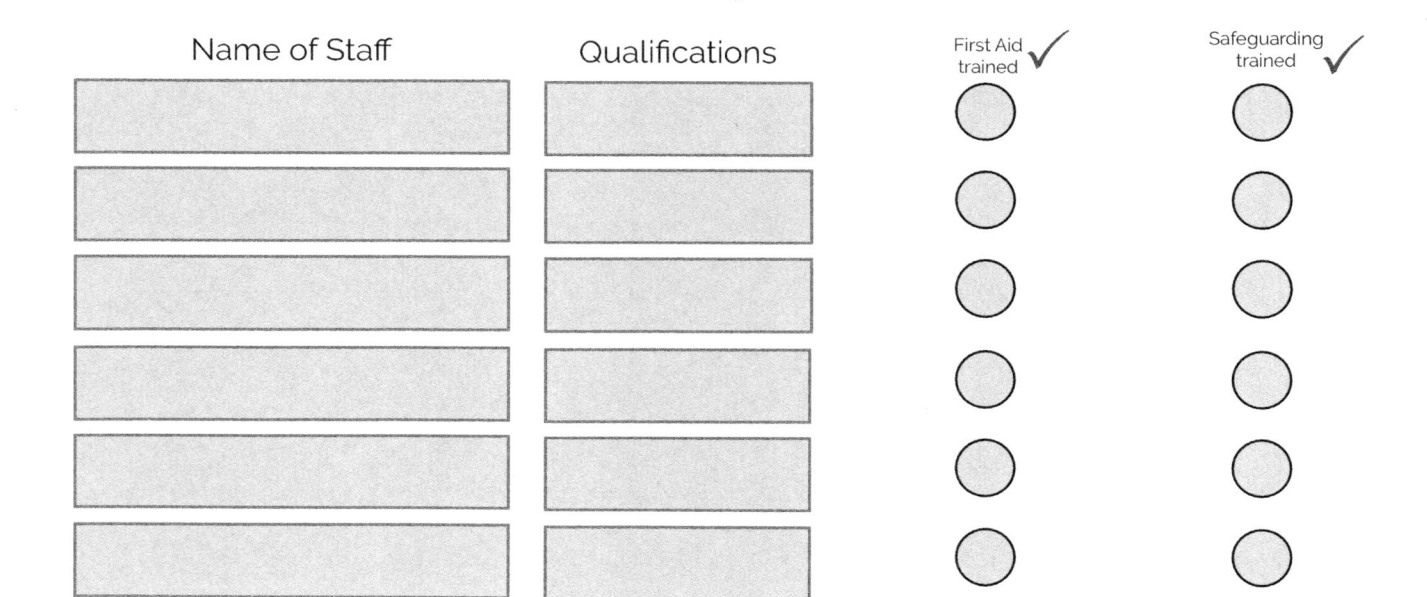

Staffing

Name of Staff	Qualifications	First Aid trained ✓	Safeguarding trained ✓
		◯	◯
		◯	◯
		◯	◯
		◯	◯
		◯	◯
		◯	◯

Printed in Great Britain
by Amazon